WORSHIP & REMEMBRANCE

WORSHIP & REMEMBRANCE

DANIEL SMITH

GOSPEL FOLIO PRESS
P. O. Box 2041, Grand Rapids MI 49501-2041

Cover design by J. B. Nicholson, Jr.

These 52 meditations and the introduction are selected from four
volumes privately published by the author as
"Worship & Remembrance, Vols. I, II, III, and IV.

Published by Gospel Folio Press
P. O. Box 2041, Grand Rapids MI 49501-2041

Gospel Folio Press ISBN 1-882701-31-3

Printed in the United States of America

To my Saviour, the Lord Jesus Christ,
and
to the saints who gather in His Name
who have shown me
through the Eternal Spirit
the delight and duty of the true worship of the Father
and the abiding values
of the great Sacrifice for poor sinners
on Calvary's cross

Contents

Foreword

I owe much, under God, to those assemblies of the Lord's people commonly called "Brethren," especially for their emphasis on the exercise of worship and the duty of participating each week in the Lord's remembrance feast. The meditations which follow are some of the fruit of this exercise of spirit which has greatly elevated my soul at times in rich communion with the Lord.

The Lord's Supper is for those who are truly born again and have the principle of grace implanted in their souls. Those who would participate are to examine themselves (1 Cor. 11:28) whether or not their soul is alive to God through the resurrection life of the Lord Jesus Christ. For believers themselves, who have such grace implanted, there must be worthy participation. The spirit is often sluggish, the mind dull, and the body lazy. It will help enliven us if we are conscious into *Whose presence* we are coming and, for this, there is need of sharp spiritual perceptions.

Let us beware of coming before God with anything akin to a careless or trifling spirit. "I will be sanctified in them that come nigh Me," says the Lord (Lev. 10:3). There needs to be "reverence and godly fear" in our approach to God (Heb. 12:28). There is no higher exercise than pure worship, and there is no meditation equal to that which focuses on the sufferings and glories of our precious Saviour. Since the sun withdrew its light, the heavens mourned in blackness, and the rocks rent in pieces when He died, consider how we should come to the remembrance of these things.

Through sixty years of preaching, I have read widely and gleaned in many fields. I am surely indebted to many for spiritual thoughts and helpful suggestions, but would have no record of them to thank them by name for help afforded. I heartily pray that these meditations, and the rich hymns accompanying, may enlarge your vision to discern the supreme excellency of God's beloved Son, and bring a new appreciation of the fact that His sufferings and death on the cross can meet all the needs of all men everywhere. The Lord's Supper is designed to seal to your heart your interest in Christ and to draw you near Him in holy communion.

I am greatly indebted to all who have helped me, for several in the family who have checked Scriptures, typed the manuscript, and corrected any errors.

May these meditations be blessed to your souls and inspire you to a new desire for the exercise of true worship. That will be my joy as well as yours. "I commend you to God, and to the word of His grace, which is able to build you up, and to give you an inheritance among all them which are sanctified" (Acts 20:32).

DANIEL SMITH
Vancouver, BC

Introduction

How amiable are Thy tabernacles, O Lord of hosts.
My soul longeth, yea, even fainteth for the courts of the Lord:
my heart and my flesh crieth out for the living God.
PSALM 84:1-2

How amiable, how lovely, is public worship! There is no sight on earth so soul-refreshing as the gathering of true believers for worship of the living God. When Israel came out of Egyptian bondage and were on the march to God's inheritance in the Promised Land, they were commanded to build a tabernacle for public worship (Ex. 25:8). There were three parts to this tabernacle: "the holy of holies," "the holy place" adjoining it, and the "outer court." It was there in the outer court that public worship was first instituted and God manifested His living presence among His people.

THE LOVELINESS OF PUBLIC WORSHIP

"How amiable!"—and why not? It is here where the most excellent of the earth gather, for this is the company of those who are spoken of as the Lord's redeemed people, His jewels, His treasure, the members of His body, His spouse. There is no age limit among them. There is no distinction of race or of social standing. They are a people who have been washed from their sins, pardoned, sanctified, justified, reconciled, adopted into the family of God. They all have

13

received new life in Christ, His resurrection life conveyed into their spirits by the Holy Spirit, and have hope of glory in the world to come. They are a people gathered from all nations, kindreds, tribes, and tongues. They are the prize and "travail of His soul," the fruit of our Lord's passion.

For my part, I must profess before the world that no society has been of so much value to my own soul. From the bottom of my heart I bless God for His worshiping people from whom I have learned the values of such worship. The Lord's presence is obviously known among such a people, and doubtless our Lord has a very high esteem for those who so honor His Son (see Mal. 3:16).

THE ORDER OF PUBLIC WORSHIP

"Praise waiteth for Thee, O God, in Zion," and, adds the Psalmist, "I will pay my vows unto the Lord now in the presence of all His people in the courts of the Lord's house, in the midst of thee, O Jerusalem. Praise ye the Lord" (Ps. 116:14, 18, 19).

In such public worship in these New Testament times, as in the Old, there are "psalms and hymns and spiritual songs," by which the Lord's people are found "singing and making melody in [the] heart to the Lord" (Eph. 5:19). This is a great exercise in uplifting the human spirit, spirits which are often beaten down by the cares of the world and our weekly toil. Such joyful song, with its sacred harmony and melody, is a sweet and comforting cordial.

Then there are the audible expressions of worship in prayer. In those gatherings with which I fellowship, men who feel liberty through the leading of the Spirit will rise and, on behalf of the whole congregation, approach "the footstool of God." There they express before the Lord the tributes of praise. The women are audibly silent, according to the teaching of 1 Corinthians 14:34 and 1 Timothy 2:8-14, although they can express, to their heart's delight, the inaudible devotion of their hearts. Silent, too, are men who feel inadequate in expression, but all are represented by those who do express themselves. We should care nothing for copious phrases and high rhetoric, which mean nothing to God, either.

There may also be short and appropriate ministry from God's Word—something suitable to the nature of the meeting and which will focus our eyes on the glory of God and the sacrifice of His beloved Son. Rich thoughts from those who can open the veins of gold and silver in Scripture, is helpful to the soul if it stirs our hearts to greater love for Him. The aim of such ministry is to excite spiritual affections and enlarge the appreciation for our Lord's Calvary sacrifice.

There is, too, in the fellowship to which I belong, an opportunity to present our material gifts to the Lord. Collections are not taken in public gatherings into which outsiders come. We take nothing from them (3 Jn. 1:7). The Lord's work is supported only by the Lord's people and nothing should be received from those who are not the Lord's. The Lord wants their hearts before their gifts.

THE MANNER OF PUBLIC WORSHIP

"My soul longeth, yea, even fainteth for the courts of the Lord: my heart and my flesh crieth out for the living God." Such desire is an insatiable yearning for the revealed presence of the Lord in His courts. "Even fainteth"—David could hardly hold out till He had met with God's people! "My heart and my flesh crieth out for the living God." He mentions His soul, his heart, his flesh, constituting the whole man. Everything a man is in himself is brought into exercise in worship. What intensity of desire is expressed by the Psalmist! One wonders at what state we have arrived in this declining age when hearts find the exercise so difficult and undesirable. O, if we could only realize the majesty of the most High God, and understand something of the love poured out in sacrifice at the cross, we might be more inclined to come and worship the Lord in "the beauty of holiness" and "in spirit and in truth."

> *Everlasting glory be,*
> *God the Father, unto Thee;*
> *'Tis with joy Thy children raise*
> *Hearts and voices in Thy praise.*

15

Thine the light that showed our sin,
Showed how guilty we had been;
Thine the love that freely gave
Thine own Son our souls to save.

Called to share the rest of God
In the Father's blest abode;
God of love and God of light,
In Thy praises we unite.

Gladly we Thy grace proclaim,
Knowing now the Father's name:
God and Father, unto Thee
Everlasting glory be!

—J. WILSON SMITH

1
The Bread Which We Break

The bread which we break, is it not the communion
of the body of Christ?
1 CORINTHIANS 10:16

As we gather at the Lord's Supper, three things are usually set
before our eyes—two on the table; one under the table. The elements
on the table are bread and wine, and that which lies under the table
is the offering bag. When the meeting is over, the bread is broken, the
cup is empty, and the bag is full. The bread is broken to symbolize
our Lord's broken body. The contents of the cup are poured out to
symbolize His poured life in the shedding of His precious blood. The
bag once empty is now full, which symbolizes the love tokens and
appreciation of His people—an offering, which should be permitted
only to those who are the Lord's people (see 1 Cor. 16:2).

As we look at the loaf, we are reminded of the words of Leviticus
21:22, "the bread of his God." These words referred to the showbread, placed fresh and warm on the table in the holy place of the
tabernacle (Ex. 25:30). As with all bread, it was made out of wheat
grain, which sprang from a cursed earth. It was then ground in a mill,
mixed with water, kneaded by the hands of man, and finally baked in
a hot oven. By this process the grain became bread fit for man's con-
sumption and the sustenance of his life. This pointed forward to our

Saviour as the true Bread of life for His redeemed people.

THE BREAD PROVIDED BY GOD

The Lord has not only redeemed His people and imparted new life through His Son, but has made provision for the sustenance and development of that new life. Life demands that! It cries out for food to sustain it and develop it. This is what bread is for in the realm of the physical, and symbolizes God's provision for us in the giving of His Son for the sustenance of our spiritual life. God provides the true Bread, His beloved Son, whose flesh was given for the life of the world (Jn. 6:51).

Our Lord speaks of Himself as the "corn of wheat" (Jn. 12:24). Such grain must pass through various processes before it becomes bread to eat. The grain must be cast into the earth where frost binds it and storms lash it. When it rises triumphant from these assaults, and multiplies in fullness, then there is the cutting down, the grinding, the kneading, and the firing of it. This points to our Lord becoming flesh, taking His place in this accursed earth, and the hardships and cruelties He bore at the hands of men, all part of the process by which He became bread prepared by God for our souls.

It was thus that He was "made perfect through suffering," and suitable to become Bread of Life to feed and satisfy His redeemed people (Heb. 2:10). We must realize that every grief He bore, every suffering endured, every buffeting at the cruel hands of men, and every change He underwent in the circumstances of His life, all was designed to fit Him to become this Bread of God to our souls.

"My Father giveth you the true bread from heaven" (Jn. 6:32), said our Lord. This chapter which speaks so much of Christ as the Bread of Life does not refer to the Lord's Supper, which was not instituted at that time. Nor do we eat His flesh and drink His blood in a carnal way, as some aver; this notion our Lord Himself rejected (Jn. 6:63). But what is spoken of is something we are to realize when we gather at the Supper. It is that spiritual exercise in which we feed on Christ.

The bread "which we break" is not necessary to salvation, for many saints died before the institution of the feast. The repentant thief on the cross did not share in it. That which is spoken of in John 6 means feeding on Christ in a spiritual manner, participating in the merits of His sufferings and death and all the benefits arising from it, for our spiritual consolation and growth. The remembrance is for the refreshing, supporting, and nourishing of our souls. Without feeding spiritually on Christ, we "have no life in [us]" (6:53), no spiritual life. But feeding on Christ is a sure sign that we are His, and desire growth and communion with Him.

In ancient times only the priests of Israel ate the showbread on the table in the tabernacle. But in the New Testament all believers are priests of God, so that the partaking of the bread is for all the Lord's people. There are some who feel that the bread on the table should be unleavened as in the Jewish passover feast, since leaven is a symbol of evil. But this is to place too much emphasis on the symbol. It is not the mere bread on the table which is acceptable to God in these days, but that which the element symbolizes—God's Beloved Son Himself. If there is leaven in the bread, then it may well serve to remind us that our Lord "was made sin for us."[1]

In the ancient symbolic rite none but the priests were to partake of the showbread. So Christ, the true Bread, is only for God's true priesthood, the company of people redeemed through His blood. The Lord's Supper, therefore, is set only for those who have been saved by His grace and have the assurance in their hearts that they have been accepted in Him. Angels have no place around this table. It is not for unrepentant sinners, who are still in a polluted state with their

1. Those who use unleavened bread are free, of course to do so. But the ordinance was designed so believers in every part of the world could participate. Some have rice bread, or manioc bread, or sourdough. The New Testament word used is simply the common word for any bread, whether leavened or unleavened. Interestingly, the Passover bread, picturing the physical body of the Lord, was unleavened, but the Pentecost bread, symbolizing the mystical body of Christ, was leavened. However it should be noted that the action of the leaven had been arrested by the fire.

19

sins. They, too, have no place here, for this exercise is a partaking of Christ in association with God, who shares our delight and appreciation in His Son.

I say "in association with God," for God is present. The bread of the tabernacle was called "showbread," which means "presence bread." It was set before the Lord in the tabernacle, where His Presence was known. God Himself finds satisfaction in the Lord Jesus, just as we should.

Israel's showbread, of necessity had to be continually removed and renewed, since it was only symbolic of living bread. But the reality of that symbol is Christ, and He abides forever. He is, and shall be, forever before the Father as His fullest delight and satisfaction. At the same time, He is all of that before His redeemed ones, and shall be that forever throughout eternity. We delight in Him, in whom the Father delights. We are satisfied with the Bread of Life, who satisfies God. We are well pleased with Him, in whom the Father is well pleased. The Lord Jesus is the Bread of God to our souls.

Thus His "flesh is meat indeed," our truly nourishing food. In partaking we are refreshed in Him as with bread, and so strengthened for spiritual warfare, duty, and suffering, being thus enabled to go on in our spiritual journey. The food for the body perishes, as do all earthly things, but Christ abides forever.

For the words that turn our eye
To the cross of Calvary,
Bidding us in faith draw nigh,
We give Thee thanks, O Lord.

Till He come we take the bread,
Type of Him on whom we feed,
Him who liveth and was dead!
We give Thee thanks, O Lord.
　　　　　　　　　　　—HORATIUS BONAR

2
The Cup Which We Drink

The cup of blessing which we bless, is it not the communion
of the blood of Christ?
1 Corinthians 10:16

In the ancient system given to Israel by God, there was, in the sacrifices, a transfer of the sinner's sin to the substitutionary victim. The sinner, accepting the sacrifice appointed by God, put his hand on the head of it and confessed his sin over it. In doing this, there was an actual legal transfer of the sinner's sin to the sacrifice. The sacrifice was then led out to die. The death due to the sinner was now by righteous law demanded of the one on whom the guilt rested. The sacrifice thus had to bear the penalty. Death alone could remove that guilt. Without the shedding of blood there could be no remission (Heb. 9:22). This all pointed in living detail to the death of the Lord Jesus and to the sacrifice He was to make on our behalf.

The Cup Which the Saviour Drank

"The cup which My Father hath given Me, shall I not drink it?" (Jn. 18:11). This was a reference to the bitterness of the sufferings of the cross—deep and fathomless—which was an agony to His holy but true humanity. In the garden of Gethsemane, the prospect of these sufferings began to press upon Him; we read that He began to be "sore amazed, and...very heavy." What profound words, remembering who He was.

The sufferings of the cross were not caused by mental disappointment, for the Lord knew from the beginning what Judas would do. Nor were His sufferings occasioned by the fear of death, for the Lord knew that He would rise again the third day. Nor, again, were they to be accounted for by the torments of Satan, whom the Lord had come to destroy.

This alone was the cause: "The cup which My Father hath given Me." He had become, through incarnation, God's righteous Servant. He served God fully, complete in His obedience. He served Him with delight, without intermission or weariness. He served Him righteously, so that "in Him [was] no sin." Yet He was given the bitterest of all cups to drink, which engaged Him in the sorest grief beyond our imagination. *God* gave Him this bitter cup to drink.

It was as though in that cup was the concentration of all human perversity, wickedness, and lawlessness. And in that cup, also, was the taste of death for every man, together with the fire and fury of God's wrath against every sin of man. It was the concentrated bitterness of all human iniquity with all the punishment it deserved. With that in His hand, so to speak, His human soul shrank from the anguish of it, and how deep were the cries expressed by Him as we see in the Messianic psalms. "My heart is sore pained within Me: and the terrors of death are fallen upon Me. Fearfulness and trembling are come upon Me, and horror hath overwhelmed Me" (Ps. 55:4-5). These are infinite sorrows, incomprehensive to our finite minds.

It is no wonder the apostle said, "It is Christ that died," as though no one ever had died but He. And in very truth this was so. For Christ our Saviour died, not only the first death, but the second death also, when He was banished from the presence of God. This death He suffered when God's face was turned away from Him. That was the essence of the bitter cup.

THE CUP WHICH BELIEVERS DRINK

"I will take the cup of salvation, and call upon the name of the

Lord" (Ps. 116:13). "The cup of blessing," Paul calls it and that it surely is. It is "better than wine" says the Song of Songs (1:2), which means better than the sweetest thing on earth. There is *pardon for sins* in it. "In whom we have redemption through His blood, the forgiveness of sins" (Eph. 1:7). This is the first sweet taste which comes to our lips as we drink the cup, and how sweet forgiveness is! Righteousness had satisfied itself with the Surety, Christ, instead of upon the actual sinner, so that God was able to proclaim righteous pardon to the condemned. The sense of this pardon comes to the sinner only by divine revelation. It cannot be known by the light of reason. The law grants no pardon and accepts no repentance. Thus pardon is found only in the gospel of the grace of God and through the merits of His Son.

There is *assurance* in it. "I know whom I have believed" (2 Tim. 1:12) says the apostle with great certainty. The bride in the Song of Songs exults in this: "My Beloved is mine, and I am His" (Song of Sol. 2:16). This sweet truth we re-echo when we sing:

> *Blessed assurance, Jesus is mine,*
> *Oh, what a foretaste of glory divine!*

How good it is, while around us men's hearts are failing them for fear (Lk. 21:26), to have assurance that it is well with our souls! This knowledge of salvation is one of the principal objects of Holy Scripture and brings the happy persuasion that we are fully accepted by God "in the Beloved" (Eph. 1:6).

There is *eternal life* in it. "I give unto them eternal life; and they shall never perish" (Jn. 10:28). Here is something which the natural man can never know, but which is tasted by true believers because of Him, who, having died and risen again, has become the Life-giver of all who believe.

There is *peace* in it. "He is our peace" (Eph. 2:14) and has made peace "through the blood of His cross." Many things are connected with this heavenly and certain peace. The sorrow of true repentance results in this peace. The understanding of the glorious truths of the gospel flow into it. The absence of fear of losing salvation or its being dissolved by death promotes it. Daily devotion to our Lord and His interest multiplies that peace.

There is *final perfection and eternal glory* in it, too. "The glory which Thou gavest Me," said our Lord, "I have given them" (Jn. 17:22). The poor heathen sorrow without hope. Death is awful gloom to them, and there is no light beyond it. For the unbeliever there is no hope, no brightness, no triumph. But for those in Christ, eternity bursts into view with all of heaven's light and glory. Thus the cup, once so bitter to the taste of our Lord, has been changed and handed to us as a "cup of blessing."

> *Till He come we take the cup;*
> *As we at His Table sup;*
> *Eye and heart are lifted up!*
> *We give Thee thanks, O Lord.*

> *For that coming, here foreshown,*
> *For that day to man unknown,*
> *For the glory and the throne,*
> *We give Thee thanks, O Lord.*

—HORATIUS BONAR

3
The Prophetic Lamb

He is brought as a lamb to the slaughter.
ISAIAH 53:7

Our Lord as the Lamb of God is the central theme of all Scripture, the one theme which makes the Scriptures a consistent whole. The heart of its message is that "Christ died for our sins." In verse 7 of this chapter there is set forth those penal, substitutionary, and expiatory sufferings arising out of the sinfulness of man, and the disposition in which our Lord suffered them. The saving of men could only be accomplished by His bearing, in our place, "the iniquity of us all." That exposed Him to the most extreme suffering and in the greatest extensity. "He was oppressed, and He was afflicted" (v. 7). He made no resistance; He showed no reluctance; this was the cause for which He came.

THE LAMB AS THE CENTRAL THEME

Until the Lord Jesus is seen as God's appointed sacrifice to purchase our redemption, the soul of man drifts hopelessly toward the shores of eternal woe. But this chapter is blazoned with the fact of Christ as the substitutionary Lamb. There are seven statements which view His sacrifice from the point of view of our human needs: (1) "He hath borne our griefs"; (2) He "carried our sorrows"; (3) "He

25

was wounded for our transgressions"; (4) "He was bruised for our iniquities"; (5) "the chastisement of our peace was upon Him"; (6) "with His stripes we are healed"; (7) "the Lord hath laid on Him the iniquity of us all." He fully paid our debt—life for life. He readily took man's place and readily met man's responsibilities. He approved the law which man had broken.

There are also seven statements which view our Lord's sacrificial death from the viewpoint of God's justice: (1) "for the transgression of My people was He stricken"; (2) "Thou shalt make His soul an offering for sin"; (3) "by His knowledge shall My righteous Servant justify many"; (4) "He shall bear their iniquities"; (5) "He was numbered with the transgressors"; (6) "He bare the sin of many"; (7) He "made intercession for the transgressors."

Between these two sevenfold differing points of view, we read in verse 7 that "He is brought as a lamb to the slaughter." That is central. The Lamb of God is in the midst where all can see Him. We must always remember this about ourselves—that "all we like sheep have gone astray; we have turned every one to his own way." We are in disgrace by our folly, rebellion, ingratitude, and disobedience. "O my God, I am ashamed and blush to lift up my face to Thee, my God; for our iniquities are increased over our head" (Ezra 9:6). But here is a sacrifice in a depth we can never probe, a height we can never reach. We wonder and adore. The sacrifice of the Lamb of God is our salvation's price.

THE LAMB AS THE STRENGTH OF GOD

He is "the arm of the Lord"—which means the omnipotent strength of God. When Moses worked a certain miracle in Egypt, the magicians acknowledged, "This is the finger of God." What is set forth here in Christ is "the arm of God." In His eternal Son, God has made bare His holy arm in the eyes of the nations. "The arm of the Lord" is that in which He displays and exerts His strength. Christ suffering, dying, and rising again is the most wonderful display of divine power ever known. It was the arm of God in Christ which was to pull down all the strongholds of the enemy and bring down every

26

high thing that had exalted itself (2 Cor. 10:5). But did it take the full strength and power of God to destroy the strongholds of Satan and rescue man from sin's tremendous woe? "He was crucified through weakness" (2 Cor 13:4)! If the greatest evidence of God's power in Christ was accomplished in weakness, how strong must He be! "The weakness of God is stronger than men" (1 Cor. 1:25).

God could not leave man in such a condition as he was, simply abandoning him to Satan, thus allowing His original intention in creating man to be defeated. God would now exert His strength, and that strength is displayed in the cross when His beloved Son bore all the weight and endured all the punishment which were due to us. Our problem in life is our transgression—our sin—our iniquity—all of which are mentioned in this chapter. It took the strength of God in Christ to bear that crushing burden. Alas, the great majority are deaf to His report of good news and blind to see the arm of God at work.

The sacrifice of the cross is never a difficulty to a truly penitent sinner. It is "the power of God unto salvation." The strength of God's arm is in its saving power. There are many who stumble at the Cross. Until they learn, by the Spirit's aid, the strength of its power and receive its message—thus proving its power in themselves—they must remain lost. The one deep, stark reality behind the Cross is that there is a real Gehenna, a real hell of torment. It is where souls are lost forever. The cross is God's method of removing the whole thing called sin, and restoring man again into His own likeness.

THE LAMB AS THE START OF A NEW CREATION

"He shall see His seed" (v. 10). In chapter 6, the prophet sees the Lord "sitting upon a throne, high and lifted up"—Christ in His exaltation. There then follow almost thirty chapters of judgments on the nations, for, as Daniel said, "the heavens do rule." But what staggers and baffles the prophet, as it does our own mind and heart, is to see this high and lofty One "brought as a lamb to the slaughter." Whoever heard of a king dying for his subjects? But these are the things of God and not the things of men.

The prophet then moves past the cross into the triumph of His res-

27

urrection. "He shall see His seed." "He shall see of the travail of His soul, and shall be satisfied" (v. 11). It means a new generation shall arise. This is the consequence of our Lord's sacrifice. After being "cut off out of the land of the living" and "His soul [made] an offering for sin"—"He shall see His seed." Christ shall have a spiritual posterity. Those who are born again of His Spirit are "His seed," His children—the product of His life-giving energy and who therefore bear His image and likeness. They are the "many" whose sins He bore. "He shall see of the travail of His soul," that is, the product of His agony, "and shall be satisfied." Because of the travail of His soul, He shall see the effect and produce of it and "be satisfied."

My Lord, my Master, at Thy feet adoring,
I see Thee bowed beneath Thy load of woe;
For me, a sinner, in Thy life-blood pouring:
For Thee, my Saviour, scarce my tears will flow.

With taunts and scoffs they mock what seems Thy weakness,
With blows and outrage adding pain to pain;
Thou art unmoved and steadfast in Thy meekness—
When I am wronged how quickly I complain.

My Lord, my Saviour, when I see Thee wearing
Upon Thy bleeding brow the crown of thorn,
Shall I for pleasure live, or shrink from bearing
Whate'er my lot may be of pain or scorn?

O Victim of Thy love! O pangs most healing!
O saving death! O wounds that I adore!
O shame most glorious! Christ, before Thee kneeling,
I pray Thee keep me Thine forevermore.

—J. BRIDAINE

4
Five Things the Lord Became

I am He that liveth, and was dead.
REVELATION 1:18

The good tidings of great joy which constitute the gospel are summed up in five things which our Lord became in order to redeem us to Himself.

HE BECAME FLESH

"The Word was made [became][1] flesh" (Jn. 1:14). "The Word" is our Lord's eternal name. As such He is the Revealer of God—the Exponent of the Godhead. He is so now; He was so in the days of His flesh; He has been so from all eternity. John 1:1 tells of His eternal existence and 1:14 that He became flesh. This is the mystery of godliness. There is no argument about it. It is "without controversy" (1 Tim. 3:16).

By His doing so, the incomprehensible became comprehensible; the inaccessible became accessible; the far off became near. He who was God took upon Him our humanity and entered the world as a lit-

1. The word "became" may be preferable to the phrase "was made" in that the latter appears to be passive, something done to the Lord, rather than done willingly by His own choice.

tle child, held in one of His creature's arms. Without ceasing to be God, and without the surrender of any divine attribute, He became man—His holiness not making Him less human; His flesh not making Him less holy.

HE BECAME POOR

"Though He was rich, yet for your sakes He became poor" (2 Cor. 8:9). This I believe to be the first meaning of Ephesians 4:9—He "descended...into the lower parts of the earth," that is, into the poorest existence possible to humankind.[1] He went through every existence of human circumstance for "in all things it behooved Him to be made like unto His brethren" (Heb. 2:17), and thus was "touched with the feeling of our infirmities" (4:15). He was rich—rich in glory—rich in the love of the Father—rich in possessions, but for us and for our salvation He became poor. See Him stooping in self-abasement to take upon Him our human nature; being born in a cattle stall; working in a carpenter's shop; living much of His life in a ghetto called Nazareth; spending His youth in a home in which the family did not believe on Him; and in His Messianic ministry knowing betrayal and denial by His own; then finally exiting by death. How poor!

HE BECAME OBEDIENT

"He...became obedient unto death, even the death of the cross" (Phil. 2:8). The Lord's way was not to make a show in the flesh. He invented no way of making Himself ridiculous, as some do. He dressed in no special garb by which to attract attention to Himself. He simply did what the Father wanted Him to do. He came into this world in the office of a Divine Servant, not to do His own will but the will of His Father in heaven. There is no humility like obedience. "To obey is better than sacrifice," said Samuel. "Lo, I come," said

2. David uses this phrase, "the lower parts of the earth," to describe his birth in Psalm 139:15—"My substance was not hid from thee, when I was made in secret, and curiously wrought in the lowest parts of the earth."

30

our Lord, "to do Thy will, O God" (Heb. 10:7). This was an altogether new experience for Him. As God, there was none higher to obey. In becoming a Servant, He became subject to the Father as God, and so "learned obedience by the things which He suffered."

HE BECAME SIN

"He hath made Him to be sin for us, who knew no sin" (2 Cor. 5:21). As He assumed the role of Sin-Bearer, all our sins were laid upon Him by an act of transference. He was the Scapegoat (*azazel*) of the Old Testament with all the sins of His people placed upon Him that He might carry them away out of sight forever (Lev. 16:8-10).

Enlightened souls could say even in that day, "My burden leaves me. The scapegoat takes it away and I am relieved." Sins were borne by the scapegoat beyond the camp, beyond all sight, beyond the track of man, to the far borders of a wild desert. There is a depth in these words which we cannot fathom. It is probably the profoundest word in Scripture, but our Lord became that in order that we might become "the righteousness of God in Him."

> *I saw a land, a solitary land,*
> *A land from every other land afar;*
> *No sun had ever kissed the gloomy strand,*
> *No dawn, nor day, nor moon, nor morning star.*

> *I saw a goat with heavy head drooped low,*
> *With sunken eye, and worn, far-travelled feet;*
> *In that sad land alone, a living woe;*
> *I heard its hoarse, forsaken, piteous bleat.*

> *It pierced the moral universe on high,*
> *Upon eternal shores the echoes brake,*
> *That lone, that loud, that lamentable cry:*
> *"My God, My God, why didst Thou Me forsake?"*[3]

---

3. From the poem "Azazel," by I. Y. Ewan, in his collection, *The Caravanserai.*

HE BECAME DEAD

"I am He that liveth, and was [became] dead" (Rev. 1:18). All those things which our Lord became were entirely voluntary and of His own will. You and I have to die; death has a claim on us. We have no choice. But death had no claim on the Son of God. He died, I believe, not the first death first, but the second death first, which is the ultimate of death—banishment from the presence of God. That was the meaning of the central cry from the cross, "My God, My God, why hast Thou forsaken Me?" (Mt. 27:46). He became dead for us, that is, He entered into death that He might destroy the power of it and "deliver them who through fear of death were all their lifetime subject to bondage" (Heb. 2:15).

The Lord was never a dying man. Death had no claim on Him. It could not put forth a clammy hand on His blessed brow. He laid down His life. He voluntarily surrendered to death that He might blast to bits the power of it and set us free.

> *I know that my Redeemer lives:*
> *What comfort this sweet sentence gives!*
> *He lives, He lives, who once was dead;*
> *He lives my everlasting Head.*
>
> *He lives to bless me with His love,*
> *And still He pleads for me above;*
> *He lives to raise me from the grave,*
> *And me eternally to save.*
>
> *He lives my mansion to prepare;*
> *And He will bring me safely there;*
> *He lives, all glory to His Name!*
> *Jesus, unchangeably the same!*

—SAMUEL MEDLEY

5

The Desire to See Jesus

Sir, we would see Jesus.

JOHN 12:21

This was the inquiry of certain Greeks, and few things stirred the heart of our Lord like the coming of these men. Maybe He saw in them a token of what would be the fruit of His sufferings from among the Gentiles. Whatever their motive—and some seem to question that, though I myself do not—the inquiry seems to embody the deep, elemental cry of our humanity. We need to see Jesus, for the idols of this world speak vanity. Its gold and silver do not satisfy; its sophistries and philosophies do not answer the deep cry of man's soul. Unless men see Jesus, they can never find rest and happiness. But how are we to see Him?

SEE HIM AS GOD

Isaiah 40 tells us that a forerunner would come to prepare the way of the Lord and that his cry would be: "Behold your God!" So the apostle John in the New Testament says, "The Word was God." The prophets of old declared the coming Messiah to be "the Mighty God" (Isa. 9:6). The New Testament apostles testified by the Spirit of God that "by Him were all things created" (Col. 1:16); that "without Him was not anything made that was made" (Jn. 1:3); that He—the Lord

Jesus Christ—was "God...manifest in the flesh" (1 Tim. 3:16). Unless Jesus was God He could not remove one stain of sin from our sin-soiled souls, nor could He save us, nor could His righteousness justify us, nor could He open the gates of heaven to us. But He *is* God—God the eternal Son. "They shall call His name Emmanuel...God with us" (Mt. 1:23). Only because He is God, "the Lord our Righteousness," is He "able to save" us (see Jer. 23:6).

SEE HIM AS MAN

Pilate set Him before the people and cried, "Behold the man!" (Jn. 19:5). "The Word was made flesh" (Jn. 1:14). Paul says that He "was made in the likeness of men" (Phil. 2:7). It is of the utmost importance to see Him as true Man, or else He would have no blood to shed for our sins; no body to give "for the life of the world" (Jn. 6:51); no Kinsman standing; no role as Mediator between God and men. He entered into our humanity that He might have a link with manhood—born of woman that He might have a link with womanhood—born a child that He might have a link with childhood. He came with a real but a new humanity: sinless, spotless, and wholly impeccable—an ideal, perfect Man upon whom alone God could put glory declaring, "This is My beloved Son, in whom I am well pleased" (Mt. 17:5).

SEE HIM AS THE LAMB

"Behold the Lamb of God, which taketh away the sin of the world" (Jn. 1:29). The Scripture assigns no other reason for which the eternal Son of God became incarnate than that He might lay down His life for His sheep—to give His life a ransom for us, to die in our place—to shed His precious blood that we might be cleansed from all sin. This is a verse which should be engraved in letters of gold on our hearts. His Godhead was not enough to redeem us. His incarnation was not enough; His power was not enough; His holiness was not enough. His sacrificial death alone was sufficient to atone for our sins. Anything which stops short of that effects nothing. Anything other than that simply mocks our need. Speaking by the psalmist of old, Messiah says, "I restored that which I took not away."

34

He did no sin, thought no sin, could not sin, but God "made Him to be sin for us, who knew no sin; that we might be made the righteousness of God in Him" (2 Cor. 5:21).

SEE HIM AS KING

"Behold your King," said Pilate (Jn. 19:14), and he said more than he knew. Though he said it in cynical scorn of the Jews, Pilate never said a truer word. The Lord Jesus is the Father's appointed King. He was sent to be King of Israel (Zech. 9:9), but Israel rejected their King. In this age, when Israel is temporarily laid aside, He reigns in the hearts of all who believe, and so establishes His kingdom within. But He is to return to earth and that to be King over all the earth, to conclude all Gentile world rule, to deliver creation from bondage, and to bring in His own kingdom of righteousness, peace, and joy over all the earth. Glorious will the day be when "the kingdoms of this world are become the kingdoms of our Lord, and of His Christ; and He shall reign for ever and ever" (Rev. 11:15).

O teach me what it meaneth—
That cross uplifted high,
With One—the Man of sorrows—
Condemned to bleed and die!

O teach me what it cost Thee
To make a sinner whole;
And teach me, Saviour, teach me
The value of a soul.

O teach me what it meaneth—
Thy love beyond compare,
The love that reacheth deeper
Than depths of self-despair!

Yes, teach me, till there gloweth
In this cold heart of mine
Some feeble, pale reflection
Of that pure love of Thine.

35

O Infinite Redeemer!
I bring no other plea,
Because Thou dost invite me
I cast myself on Thee.

Because Thou dost accept me
I love and I adore;
Because Thy love constraineth,
I'll praise Thee evermore.

—LUCY A. BENNETT

6
The Death of Christ

Christ died for our sins according to the Scriptures.
1 CORINTHIANS 15:3

The death of the Lord Jesus Christ is the first fact of the gospel of His grace. Its interpretation is the first work of Christian teaching. It is through this sacrificial and substitutionary death of the Lord Jesus that peace can be given to a burdened conscience, fetters of sin be broken, the blight of the hereditary curse be cut off, the spirit of adoption be given, and a new sense of life and power be imparted to sinful men. But experience demands explanation. Doctrine is the inevitable ground of experience. Faith must be assured, and it can be assured only by biblical explanation and authority.

PROPHETICALLY

The Old Testament prepares us for the New. It does so by presenting the foreordained death of the Son of God by both picture and promise. There are many vivid pictures or types of His death, such as the offering of Isaac (Gen. 22:1-14); the Day of Atonement (Ex. 30:10); the red heifer (Num. 19:1-10); the brazen serpent (Num. 21:1-9); and all the Levitical offerings through centuries of time.

Then, secondly, by promises. The Old Testament is as laden with promises as it is with pictures. I mention three or four only. Genesis

3:15 presents the Seed of the woman which was to bruise Satan's head. This was a promise to the first man and woman, following their fall into sin, that One would come who would be the Seed of the woman. This is a strange departure from the course of nature, for all the children of those first parents are the seed of the man. This is a glorious exception so that this One would avoid the contamination of human sin.

Psalm 22 is one of the great Messianic psalms. The opening words are those used by our Lord on the cross: "My God, My God, why hast Thou forsaken Me?" There are matters in this psalm which could never apply to David, the writer, nor to the nation of Israel. In verse 16, we read: "They pierced My hands and My feet," which indicates crucifixion. This method of death, however, was unknown in those days. Seven hundred years after the writing of Psalm 22, it was a Roman-inaugurated manner of death, whereas the Jewish method was stoning. The psalm finishes with this word: "He hath done this," which is the same as the Lord's word on the cross, "It is finished."

The promise of Isaiah 53 speaks of the One who is to come who will bear the sins of others: "He was wounded for our transgressions, He was bruised for our iniquities" (v. 5). His sacrificial death was to be substitutionary, since we are told in verse 6: "The Lord hath laid on Him the iniquity of us all."

Zechariah 13:7 declares, "Awake, O sword, against My shepherd, and against the man that is My fellow, saith the Lord of hosts." The word "fellow" means equal. This tells us that the One to come is co-equal with God.

Such are some of the expressive pictures and promises of the Old Testament as the prophets prophesied "beforehand the sufferings of Christ" (1 Pet. 1:11).

HISTORICALLY

From the Old Testament we may now move into the pages of the Gospels in the New Testament. We offer these three observations:

Personally, the death of Christ was a mystery. Through the medium of our humanity, our Lord became true man. In that humanity our

sins were, at a point of time, transferred to Him. He is thus presented as taking the place of sinners in His death, but how the Son of God
could enter into death is beyond our reasoning. We can understand
how it was that, as our Representative, He had to die: where the guilt
lay, there the penalty must fall. But how that One who was the incor-
ruptible God could, as the Son of man, enter into the mystery of
death, is itself the greatest of all mysteries.

Humanly, the death of Christ was a tragedy. We read that in His
earthly life He "went about doing good." His open hands literally dis-
pensed a sea of blessings to poor specimens of our humanity—the
blind, deaf, dumb, leprous, paralyzed, and even the dead. Yet it was
men of our humanity, and the most religious and civilized part of it
at that, who transfixed Him to a cross. Peter charged that they had
"killed the Prince of life." Stephen called them murderers. The evil
of men came out at the cross, and that evil could be expressed thus,
"This is the heir; come, let us kill Him."

Divinely, the death of Christ was a ministry. It was the only means
of man's redemption. Thus it was by "the determinate counsel and
foreknowledge of God." God was at work in the transaction of the
cross, "reconciling the world unto Himself." God was in Christ, not
against Him. The death of Christ is the fullest revelation of God as
the God of all grace. It is love stronger than shame, suffering, and
death. It is love immeasurable, unquenchable. It was love being put
to the most extreme test, and love proving triumphant. Here is the
righteousness of God meeting the unrighteousness of men and finding a means whereby God could be just, yet the Justifier of the
ungodly.

EXPERIENTIALLY

The Old Testament prepares us for the cross; the Gospels present
that cross with the death of the blessed Son of God upon it; and now
the Acts of the Apostles proclaims that death. Experience is the key
to its meaning. The death of the Lord Jesus is the foundation of the
Christian gospel. The substance of apostolic teaching was that
"Christ died for our sins according to the Scriptures." Nothing else

can deal with the sin of man's soul or give him hope for eternity.

When the Apostle Paul went into the voluptuous city of Corinth, he determined to know nothing among them but "Christ, and Him crucified." Nothing else could meet the power of sin and overcome it. Instead of keeping the cross hidden, the apostle declared it. The cross of Christ was the heart and life of the gospel, and the apostle set it forth so that all men could see the truth of it.

"Christ died for our sins." That is all-inclusive and the one and final interpretation of the death of the Lord Jesus Christ on Calvary's cross. The plain fact of the gospel is that the Lord Jesus, dying on behalf of sinners, can save sinners. This is not the fancies of a religious cult, but the gospel of man's redemption. There is power in the cross to save, and this is what is proclaimed in the Acts of the Apostles. Such a salvation becomes a reality to men when, by spiritual illumination, they realize that Christ died for me...He loved me...He gave Himself for me!

"Man of Sorrows, What a name
For the Son of God, who came,
Ruined sinners to reclaim.
Hallelujah! what a Saviour!

Bearing shame and scoffing rude,
In my place condemned He stood;
Sealed my pardon with His blood;
Hallelujah! what a Saviour!

—PHILLIP P. BLISS

7

The Agonies of Golgotha

*The sorrows of death compassed me, and the floods of ungodly men
made me afraid. The sorrows of hell compassed me about: the
snares of death prevented me. In my distress I called upon the Lord,
and cried unto my God: He heard my voice out of His temple, and
my cry came before Him, even into His ears.*
PSALM 18:4-6

There is no doubt that this is a Messianic Psalm. There is a depth
of suffering and a completeness of deliverance which have no par-
allel in David's personal life, nor in the life of any other Old
Testament saint. We must refer these verses to our Lord, and the Lord
Himself may have made reference to this very psalm when He said
in Luke 24:44, "All things must be fulfilled, which were written…in
the Psalms concerning Me."

THE LORD'S AGONY IN HIS SUFFERINGS

The sufferings of our Lord were not caused by any personal physical infirmity or disease. They were not from within His own body
but were inflicted from without. He was taken, and by wicked hands
was crucified and slain (Acts 2:23). The scourging which He endured
was so brutal as to often lift the whole skin from its victims and
expose their inner organs. The pummeling He received from wicked

41

men and the pulling out of His beard must have been excruciating. And who can tell what is meant by such expressions as "the sorrows of death"—"the floods of ungodly men"—"the sorrows of hell"— "the snares of death"? It was not only that He was compassed around by the basest of our humanity but also attacked by the whole hierarchy of hell. "Floods" means torrents, and torrent after torrent of the most fierce and violent assault was thrown against our Lord. Then to be bound by the cords from which there could be no escape but by the almighty power of Deity, must have been truly alarming. All this constitutes the agony of the God-man, our Saviour. He underwent every pang which would have tortured His redeemed if they had been tossed into the flames of hell forever.

The cross of Christ is an awful scene. We can only survey it in the calm of holy reverence. The sufferings which He endured both in physical pain, mental anguish, and spiritual distress, are far beyond our understanding. Those sufferings were involved in paying our ransom price, effecting our escape. They are the means of rescue from eternal ruin. All those terrible sufferings died in our Lord and cannot revive to injure or hurt His people. We do well to "consider Him," and never to forget what He suffered on our behalf. He died "the Just for the unjust"; was "wounded for our transgressions"; "bruised for our iniquities"; and thus "the chastisement of our peace was upon Him." He bore "our sins in His own body on the tree" (1 Pet. 2:24).

THE LORD'S PRAYERS IN HIS SUFFERINGS

"In My distress I called upon the Lord, and cried unto My God" (Ps. 18:6). The Lord was no Stoic, nor did He adopt a stoical attitude to these appointed sufferings. In His distress He sought God. "I cried unto My God," and, we read, He "was heard in that He feared" (Heb. 5:7). Wherever the Lord is, a praying voice is heard. His first and last look is toward heaven. His life on earth as the Son of man and the divine Servant was one flow of prayer. And now, in this hour of supreme sacrifice, His hope, His trust is in God.

The Psalms are full of His cries, for He "offered up prayers and supplications, with strong crying and tears unto Him that was able to save Him from [out of] death" (Heb. 5:7). Listen to these heart rending cries: "Be not Thou far from Me, O Lord: O My strength, haste Thee to help Me. Deliver My soul from the sword; My darling from the power of the dog. Save Me from the lion's mouth" (Ps. 22:19-21). "Withhold not Thou Thy tender mercies from Me, O Lord: let Thy lovingkindness and Thy truth continually preserve Me. For innumerable evils have compassed Me about...Be pleased, O Lord, to deliver Me: O Lord, make haste to help Me" (Ps. 40:11-13). "Deliver Me out of the mire, and let Me not sink: let Me be delivered from them that hate Me, and out of the deep waters. Let not the waterflood overflow Me, neither let the deep swallow Me up, and let not the pit shut her mouth upon Me'" (Ps. 69:14-15).

Such were some of the deep, heart-rending prayers of our Lord given by the Spirit of God to the Psalmist in the spirit of prophecy. When we come to Gethsemane's garden in the New Testament, we hear the same sorrowful utterances. "O My Father, if it be possible, let this cup pass from Me: nevertheless, not as I will, but as Thou wilt...O My Father, if this cup may not pass away from Me, except I drink it, Thy will be done" (Mt. 26:39, 42). We can only tread that ground with reverent step. It is most holy. In His distress, our Lord sought relief.

THE LORD'S COMFORT IN HIS SUFFERINGS

"He heard My voice out of His temple, and My cry came before Him, even into His ears" (Ps. 18:6). His cries found no response from earth, but they were heard in heaven in the temple of God the Father. His prayers were heard and answered. The verses which follow—awesome, indeed frightful to the wicked—were the proof God had heard His cries and would both vindicate His Son and recompense His enemies for their cruelties. With the comfort of having been heard, the Lord was enabled to fling off all who assaulted Him at the cross, triumphing over them (Col. 2:15). It was no easy work to rescue souls from Satan's grasp or to lay low the prison house of darkness. The enemy flung all he had into the fight, clad in his fiercest armor, wild in his keenest rage, wily in his deadliest crafts. But, oh,

43

the Lord conquered all! Oh, what an excellent Saviour! Oh, excellent Cross! What a victory! Glorious is the Lord our God who accomplished such a perfect redemption!

Amazing, holy mystery,
Unfathomed Sacrifice,
Where incarnate Love on Calvary's tree,
Accursed for sinners, dies!
From His soul, poured out unto death, that cry
Utters sorrow and love unknown,
"Eli, Eli, lama sabachthani?"
O Sufferer, so wounded, so lone!

How couldst Thou—bruised, like a crushed worm—
Trod down in the dust of death
O'er that scene of wrathful gloom and storm
Pour love's sweet undying breath?
'Twas that doom that wrung from Thy soul the plea,
Out of depths of the direful cross,
"My God, O why hast Thou forsaken Me?"
Forsaken, blest Saviour, for us.

For us Thy scars Thou wearest still—
Sweet mark of our Advocate!
Soon Thy form of love our souls shall thrill,
Low bowed at Thy nail-pierced feet!
How Thy wounds shall speak! How Thy soul's deep cry
Shall in echo forever fall,
"Eli, Eli, lama sabachthani?"
Lord Jesus! our Glory, our All!

—FRANK ALLABEN

8

The Kinsman Redeemer

*If thy brother be waxen poor, and hath sold away some of his
possession, and if any of his kin come to redeem it, then shall he
redeem that which his brother sold.*

LEVITICUS 25:25

There was a "right of redemption" in the laws of ancient Israel. It
was there by divine arrangement. It was given to prevent the covetous
from adding field to field and land to land. If, because of stringent
circumstances, a man had to sell his land for a time, this law gave
him the right to redeem it when he was able. If such a man suddenly
grew rich, he could pay the creditor the income until the year of
jubilee and take immediate possession. But if he was not able to do
this, then "any of his kin," who was willing and able to pay the
redemption price and thus restore the lost possession to his kin, could
do so. This kinsman had to come forward to do this, which implied
his willingness and desire. There are a few thoughts arising from this
which would direct our attention to the Lord Jesus Christ.

THE KINSMAN

It was necessary for the Lord to become a kinsman of our race.
This was essential in order to gain the right to redeem and to pay the
price of redemption. He could not redeem as God alone. Infinite dis-

45

tance separates the divine and human natures. One sits enthroned in heaven's glory; the other walks on earth. It was necessary, therefore, that the Lord come into our sphere of things and take up His abode here on the planet. Thus it was that "the Word was made flesh" (Jn. 1:14). He took upon Him our human nature, and was made bone of our bone and flesh of our flesh (Eph. 5:30). "Forasmuch then as the children are partakers of flesh and blood, He also Himself likewise took part of the same" (Heb. 2:14).

In this flesh the Lord Jesus was given human names or titles. The names "Jesus," "Christ," "Immanuel," are all connected with His life here on earth. It was His incarnation which linked God and man together in His Person. While His deity was always present, His soul was truly human, not superhuman or celestial, and His body was of the very substance of His virgin mother, Mary. His was true but holy flesh, the flesh not making Him less the eternal Son of God, or making Him less holy than He was before coming into it.

Thus did the blessed Saviour make Himself a true Kinsman of our race. Becoming such, He gained the right to redeem; and the right to redeem not only the persons of our humanity, but the earth itself.

THE KINSMAN REDEMPTION PRICE

The kinsman must have more than ties of family. In His marvelous coming into our human nature, the Lord kindled the hope of redemption but did not bring redemption itself. His incarnation was only the beginning of a new hope for the poor sons of men who had lost their heavenly inheritance. But by entering into this arena the Lord was confronted with great opposing forces. The law had its own righteous demands. The fact—glorious though it was—of the coming of the Son of God into our humanity was not sufficient in itself to procure redemption. Anything which was less than the price of redemption could effect nothing. There is therefore no redemption in Bethlehem's cradle—only the hope of it. However near God might come to man, He could not redeem without the price of redemption.

The price was death, for man had sinned and the law decreed that "the soul that sinneth, it shall die" (Ezek. 18:4). Hence there must be, on the part of the Kinsman, a pouring out of His soul unto death. That is the only price by which redemption could be had. He would have to "taste death for every man," since every man had lost his possession. Who, therefore, could measure redemption's price? The Lord our Saviour must die for millions in that one death.

His body given, His blood shed—such was the price. Gold and silver were of no value in this matter. No storehouses of earth could be sufficient. Behind our Lord's humanity there was a divine nature which supplied the sufficiency, for His death was no common death. Even though the price of sin was enormous, what our Lord paid far exceeds. The right to redeem, the sufficiency to redeem, lay in the perfect nature of Him who was Son of God, and in His death on behalf of all. His offering was a divine as well as a human offering. Thus He died "the Just for the unjust," dying the sinner's death, and bearing the sinner's curse. Death could do what life, even in all its divine omnipotence, could not accomplish.

This then, is the Man with the bruised heel (Gen. 3:15). He it is to whom Abel's sacrifice pointed. It is He who emerges like a sweet savor, out of all Israel's ancient Levitical sacrifices. It is He of whom all the prophets spoke, as when Isaiah cried: "When Thou shalt make His soul an offering for sin, He shall see His seed, He shall prolong His days" (Isa. 53:10). It is He to whom, at the end of human history, is ascribed the salvation of all the redeemed in heaven: "Thou...hast redeemed us to God by Thy blood" (Rev. 5:9).

THE KINSMAN'S REDEEMED PEOPLE

"If thy brother be waxen poor." None can value this restoring grace but those who realize their penury. None of us can even restore the "overplus," as was said of the poor of Israel—that is, too poor not only to buy back but to make the least contribution to regain what he had lost. Sinners are just that poor. Who but the enlightened by the Spirit know how poor and beggarly they are? Sinful men dress themselves in gaudy apparel, and this makes them feel like royal personages. Therefore they become deluded about their condition before God. The great majority of men count their tinsel as gold; their gold

47

as abiding treasure. Alas, how blind nature is! No beggar was ever so poor as a sinful man.

Isaiah was singularly honored with clear and comprehensive views of the person and character of the Messiah, and by the Spirit of God predicted His incarnation and the final establishment of His kingdom here on earth. He tells of seeing "the Lord sitting upon a throne, high and lifted up," to whom all in heaven gave their most profound worship. But in the light of that vision, the great prophet cried, "Woe is me! for I am undone; because I am a man of unclean lips" (Isa. 6:5). In that light be discovered the utter pollution of his own personal life. It filled him with self-loathing as such a vision also did for Job when he cried, "I abhor myself, and repent in dust and ashes" (Job 42:6). That is what is meant by a sense of spiritual poverty and utter bankruptcy before God.

But the Lord came to redeem such sinners. May He give us a true apprehension of His tremendous act of self-denial in coming into our humanity, and then, in order to pay redemption's price, of stooping to the mystery of death in order to restore to us our lost inheritance.

Lord Jesus, my Saviour!
How vast Thy love to me!
I bathe in its full ocean
To all eternity;
And wending on to glory
This all my song shall be,
I am a feeble sinner,
But Jesus died for me.

In glory, in glory,
Forever with the Lord,
I'll tune my harp, and with the saints
I'll sing with sweet accord;
And as I strike the golden strings,
This all my song shall be,
I was a feeble sinner,
But Jesus died for me. —AUTHOR UNKNOWN

9
Worship—Symbolic or Spiritual?

The hour cometh, and now is, when the true worshipers
shall worship the Father in spirit and in truth:
for the Father seeketh such to worship Him.
JOHN 4:23

The reason for writing the Epistle to the Hebrews was to convince those Hebrews professing faith in the Lord Jesus that the ritualistic and ceremonial ways of approaching God had passed away. The ritualistic form of things was a grand spectacle with its beautiful temple, gorgeous robes, priests and sacrifices, singers and choirs.

It was a God-ordained system for that particular dispensation. It was full of color and music, heavy with incense, a sight fascinating to the senses. It was hard for the Hebrews to believe that all that had passed away, that the Lord had forsaken the temple in Jerusalem, that He no longer regarded Jewish priests and sacrifices, that the institutions of Moses had lost their usefulness.

THE RITUALISTIC WORSHIP

This ritualistic and symbolic form was that which the woman of Samaria referred to as she conversed with our Lord at the well of Sychar. "Our fathers worshiped in this mountain; and ye say, that in

49

Jerusalem is the place where men ought to worship" (Jn. 4:20).

She may have been evading a conscience awakened to her sinful life, but she was also genuinely groping for the true meaning of worship. She knew a form of worship—a form "in this mountain" and another form "at Jerusalem." In both places (one God-ordained, one man-ordained) there were trappings related to God's appointed way to approach Him in that dispensation. That form had its temples, its priests, its sacrifices, its altars, its incense, its vestments. When the woman said, "Our fathers worshiped in this mountain" (Mount Gerizim), she may have been referring to Abraham and Jacob, both of whom erected altars in Samaria.

Thus both in Samaria and in Jerusalem there was that which was known as worship. In this worship there was recognition of the true and living God, that He was worthy of worship, and that such worship could only be offered through the priests and sacrifices appointed by God. The priests' were His ministers especially set apart to serve Him and His people. It was all a very precious rite, and it was all symbolic of the Saviour's worth. It taught that His shed blood was necessary to approach God. The altar taught the cross. The shed blood was prefigured in the atoning sacrifice.

SPIRITUAL WORSHIP

The Lord Jesus then said to the woman, "Woman, believe Me, the hour cometh, when ye shall neither in this mountain, nor yet at Jerusalem, worship the Father...But the hour cometh, and now is, when the true worshipers shall worship the Father in spirit and in truth: for the Father seeketh such to worship Him. God is a Spirit: and they that worship Him must worship Him in spirit and in truth" (Jn. 4:21, 23-24).

The hour for true worship had come. The symbolic worship thus ended; it was done away. He to whom all symbols pointed had now come. Believers now must look to Him. They had seen animal victims die, without number. Each drop of blood from those sacrifices pointed forward to the Lamb of God. They had their witnessing priests who spared not the innocent animals, striking the death blow.

The blazing fires on the altars witnessed the consuming of their prey. His people were shown in symbol that in sacrifice all demands of wrath were met.

But when the Son of God hung, curse-bearing, on the tree, reality was set before them. Guilt was taken away, and sinners were ransomed by the Lord's anguish. The hour had come. The shadows and symbols had passed. The hour had struck for the reality of worship.

This was a new worship—not ceremonial, but spiritual. The new worship was true worship. And the Lord Jesus told the woman of Samaria three times that true worship was the worship of the Father. From the cross onward, there was to be an age when the Father would seek true worshipers.

The Father! No such name for God had ever been given Israel. He was to them Elohim, the God of power; El Shaddai, the God of provision; Jehovah, the God of promise; El Elyon, the God of preservation—but never Father. The approach to God as Father, and the worship of Him as Father, only became possible through the coming of His Son, the completion of the redemptive sacrifice, and the impartation of the Holy Spirit, who would enable true worship. This kind of worship stands in contrast to what was in Israel, a worship which at best was incomplete and in shadow.

May we, then, worship the Son through the enabling of the indwelling Spirit? Yes, we may! The Father Himself has desired that, "All men should honor the Son, even as they honor the Father" (Jn. 5:23). For further verification of this, we are given a view of heaven in Revelation 5, where both the Father and the Son are joint objects of worship. "Blessing, and honor, and glory, and power, be unto Him that sitteth upon the throne, and unto the Lamb for ever and ever" (Rev. 5:13). The Lamb, who was slain, shares the worship due only to God, because He is God—God the Son.

Father, we worship Thee,
Thro' Thy beloved Son;
And, by the Spirit, now draw near
Before Thy holy throne.

We bless Thee Thou art love,
How vast that matchless grace,
Whose breadth and length and height and depth
No finite mind can trace.

For what Thou art, we praise,
And worship, and adore:
To Father, Son, and Spirit be
The glory evermore.

—ALFRED P. GIBBS

Special Savings for New Members...

RENEW NOW AND SAVE NEARLY 30%!

As a new member, you can renew your Society membership for the special rate of just $24. It's like getting three issues of NATIONAL GEOGRAPHIC for free! Return the enclosed Renewal Form today with your payment... and save $10 off the regular membership rate of $34!

RRNG02-FL01G7

♻ Recycled paper

10
Discerning the Lord's Body

For he that eateth and drinketh unworthily, eateth and drinketh
[judgment] to himself, not discerning the Lord's body.
1 CORINTHIANS 11:29

The text means that some bring ruin on themselves because they
do not have a proper sense of the Lord's body. There is a wide diver-
gence both of thought and practice in regard to the Remembrance
feast. Apart from the mass, which is idolatrous, there is the excessive
practice of it by others by using it for varied occasions to sanctify
their own activities. There is the practice of observing it but four
times a year, or once a month. But the evidence of Scripture is that
the saints gather every Lord's Day for worship, the central feature of
which is the breaking of bread (Acts 20:7).

Perhaps a greater danger than irregularity is turning the feast into
a religious ritual and observing it without spiritual affections or any
heart exercise of worship. In Scripture, this feast is nowhere called a
sacrifice. The sacrifice for sins was once made on Calvary's cross
and is never to be repeated. But its memory is preserved in the weekly observance of the memorial feast. The gathering place for this
feast is around a table, not an altar.

The blessing of the feast is given to the participant who comes
with a proper spirit of worship, praise, and thanksgiving. There is no

priest presiding. The Lord Himself presides. Blessing is given as the participant discerns, by the Spirit's enlightenment, the spiritual realities of the ordinance. The one thing to be supremely discerned is the Lord's body, and He possesses both a personal and mystical body.

THE PERSONAL BODY OF OUR LORD

This personal body of His was crucified. The world may look on the Lord as a great moral teacher with ideals to embrace, or of a martyr dying for a cause. But true believers discern that He "bare our sins in His own body on the tree" (1 Pet. 2:24). The heart of the gospel message is not example but expiation—that He purges our sins—that in His body He "suffered for sins, the Just for the unjust, that He might bring us to God" (1 Pet. 3:18).

We also discern the same crucified body, risen and glorified. The Church is indwelt by the Holy Spirit, but the Lord Jesus lives in His glorified body before the Father's face, acting as Advocate on behalf of His people. He is not in the loaf of bread on the table as a kind of imprisoned deity. That is pagan idolatry.

Then, too, we discern His body as the body in which He will come again. "As often as ye eat this bread, and drink this cup, ye do show the Lord's death till He come" (1 Cor. 11:26). God has a great purpose concerning the material creation in our Lord's coming. He is to reclaim the earth for the "earth is the Lord's," both by creative and redemptive rights. Our material bodies will be resurrected and changed to be like "His glorious body."

THE MYSTICAL BODY OF OUR LORD

If we come to the feast with a discerning and anointed spirit, we shall recognize His mystical body in the one loaf. "We being many are one bread, and one body" (1 Cor. 10:17). The Church is His mystical body.

1. It is a body called out of this world. Believers are the *ekklesia,* a called-out people. Just as Abraham was called out of Ur of the Chaldees and Israel was called out of Egypt, so the Church is called out of a condemned world. It is distinct from the world by the expe-

rience of redemption. Believers are separated *from* the world and *to* Christ. If we by grace are brought into the most intimate union with our Lord, how can we be joined to, and intimate with, the world which crucified Him? Fellowship at the Lord's memorial feast demands separation from the world.

2. It is a body called into togetherness. "We being many are...one body" (1 Cor. 10:17). We must discern the vital bond which binds together all the redeemed. The Church is a living organism and the basis of fellowship is a common life in Christ—the life of His Spirit. We should never come to this feast while at variance with another or else our testimony ceases to be vital. All antagonism, grievances, and despising must be laid aside before partaking.

3. It is a body called unto glory. There are pessimists and skeptics who harp on the Church being a spent force and in decline. This memorial feast is to remind us every week that the company of the Lord's people is to be a most "glorious church, not having spot, or wrinkle, or any such thing; but that it should be holy and without blemish" (Eph. 5:27). This elect company, called out of "every kindred, and tongue, and people, and nation," will be together around the throne of God and of the Lamb, singing to Him who "wast slain, and hast redeemed us to God by Thy blood"—yes, singing to Him "that loved us, and washed us from our sins in His own blood" (Rev. 5:9; 1:5). We are called unto His "eternal glory."

> *O Love, how deep, how broad, how high!*
> *It fills the heart with ecstasy,*
> *That God, the Son of God, should take*
> *Our mortal form, for mortals' sake.*
>
> *For us He was baptized and bore*
> *His holy fast, and hungered sore;*
> *For us temptation sharp He knew,*
> *For us the tempter overthrew.*
>
> *For us to wicked men betrayed,*
> *Scourged, mocked, in purple robe arrayed,*

He bore the shameful cross and death,
For us at length gave up His breath.

For us He rose from death again;
For us He went on high to reign;
For us He sent the Spirit here
To guide, to strengthen, and to cheer.

—ANONYMOUS, FROM THE 15TH CENTURY
TRANSLATED BY BENJAMIN WEBB

11
The Blood of Jesus

The blood of Jesus Christ His Son.
1 JOHN 1:7

The blood of Jesus Christ has become an unpopular subject to modern preachers. I recall that, many years ago in England, a certain minister, who made quite a name for himself by his books, called reference to the blood of Jesus "a gospel of the shambles, offensive both to public taste and divine truth." No doubt he was concerned more with public taste than with divine truth, for no fact is more embedded in the Scriptures than the blood of Christ. In it lies the hidden mystery of the gospel of the grace of God. It is God's answer to man's need and must be given central place in all evangelical preaching and experience.

WHAT THE BLOOD OF JESUS IS

The first revelation in Scripture concerning the blood was that life was in it (Gen. 9:4-6). Blood, therefore, was the symbol of life. There is nothing we can add today to the ancient Scripture that "the life of the flesh is in the blood" (Lev. 17:11). Modern research only confirms the mysterious relationship between the blood and the life.

The second revelation is that the blood, holding the life, was sacred. The sacredness of life made the blood sacred. It was neither

57

to be eaten nor drunk, but poured out as a sign that life was returnable to God. When the life was released from the blood, it returned to God who gave it.

The third revelation was that the blood was to be used on the altar of sacrifice. In ancient times, sacrificial animals appointed by God, though belonging to a fallen creation were seen as sinless, not having moral capability. In this way the blood of such innocent animals was used as a figure of the precious blood of Christ, and was offered in those earlier times as a "cover" for sin. Thus if an Israelite was conscious of sin, he would bring to the tabernacle a sacrificial animal, put his hands upon it as a sign of the transference of his sin, and the animal would be slain. Its blood would then be poured out into a vessel, carried by the priest into the holy place, and sprinkled there. The body of this innocent animal was then burnt to ashes as a sign that sin had been fully judged and forgiven by its death. The blood sprinkled in the holy place spoke to God of a sinless life poured out on behalf of the sinner. Thus a righteous basis was given to God whereby He could forgive sin and accept the sinner.

It is necessary to see this if we are to understand the meaning of the blood of Christ. The blood of the sacrificial animal was its life. The blood of Christ was His life. In Him was the life of God, boundless and eternal. When the Son of God became Son of man, that life was locked up, as it were, in His blood. When He died, He fulfilled what all former sacrifices portrayed in figure. He bore our sins in His own body and suffered the righteous judgment of God on sin. But through that same death our Lord's life was released to God, and He lives before God as a sign that all sin has been answered by His atoning death. His death did not "cover" sin only, as did the ancient sacrifices, but took it away, completely removing it.

Released from death and overcoming it, our Lord now lives by the power of an endless life as the ground of our acceptance before God.

WHAT THE BLOOD OF JESUS DOES

It is important to see that the blood of Christ was shed for sin and sin only. It is the one divinely ordained means for dealing with sin. It is the most wonderful thing in all the universe.

The blood of Jesus *makes us righteous* before God: "Being now justified by His blood" (Romans 5:9). As sinners our lives are unacceptable to God. But the spotless life of God's beloved Son is wholly acceptable. Being offered on our behalf, it answers for all our sin, so that we are made acceptable to God.

The blood of Jesus *reconciles us* to God: "But now in Christ Jesus ye who sometimes were far off are made nigh by the blood of Christ" (Eph. 2:13). The blood deals with the only thing which is capable of separating us from God—sin. The efficacy of that blood is so great that we can enter into the holiest of all, where God's real presence is, and we can do so with confidence.

The blood of Jesus *gives peace* to our hearts and consciences: "Having made peace through the blood of His cross" (Col. 1:20). No longer is there any enmity between, nor any unhappy fears of God left in the believer. Our guilt is removed by the blood, and the Holy Spirit dwells within.

The blood of Jesus *redeems and sanctifies us*: "Ye were not redeemed with corruptible things...but with the precious blood of Christ" (1 Pet. 1:18-19). "Wherefore Jesus also, that He might sanctify the people with His own blood, suffered without the gate" (Heb. 13:12). The blood of Christ is the purchase price by which we are bought out of the slave market of sin and by which we are separated to God. How costly our redemption! How deep must have been the separation which took the blood of God's Son to restore us!

The blood of Jesus *cleanses us*. "The blood of Jesus Christ His Son cleanseth us from all sin" (1 Jn. 1:7). Sin makes a stain. It is a form of pollution so offensive to God that He can have no fellowship with us until it is removed. And only the blood of Christ can remove it. It does so, and makes the believer completely clean.

The blood of Jesus *gives victory* over Satan. "They overcame him by the blood of the Lamb" (Rev. 12:11). The Christian life would be valueless if there was no victory over Satan. But there is victory! The blood of Christ deals with that which gives Satan his base of operation against us. When we repent and trust the blood of Christ to cleanse, Satan must depart from us, defeated by divine power.

But what does all this mean in our experience? There are times when believers are stale, sluggish, and lifeless before God. They are not free to worship; they lose the joy of His salvation. It is important that truth work out in experience. Why then do so many believers lack a close, enjoyable walk with God? Since sin is the only separating agency, there must be sin hidden in secret places. There must be some sort of defilement. We are so slow to repent; and where there is no repentance, there can be no forgiveness. We need to come to our Lord again and again for daily cleansing. When we do so, then faith enters into all that the precious blood of Christ has secured for us, and the heart soon abounds with joy in renewed fellowship with God.

Precious, precious blood of Jesus,
Shed on Calvary;
Shed for rebels, shed for sinners,
Shed for me.

Precious blood, that has redeemed us!
All the price is paid:
Perfect pardon now is offered,
Peace is made.

Now the holiest with boldness
We may enter in;
For the open fountain cleanses
From all sin.

Precious blood, whose full atonement
Makes us near to God!
Precious blood, our way to glory,
Praise and laud.

—FRANCES R. HAVERGAL

60

12
The Hymn Sung

And when they had sung an hymn,
they went out into the mount of Olives.
MATTHEW 26:30

"Know ye what a hymn is? It is a song with praise of God. If thou praisest God and singest not, thou utterest no hymn. If thou singest and praisest not God, thou utterest no hymn. A hymn, then, containeth these three things: song, and praise, and that of God. Praise, then, of God in song is called a hymn." Such was Augustine's definition of a hymn.

A hymn is singable praise of God, a salute in song to the greatness of God and to the events of His grace which constitute the gospel. It is a combination of divine truth and Christian experience. The Psalms especially pervade many Christian hymns and have illuminated the way for Christian hymn writing. But the Scriptures themselves as a whole are the creator and molder of hymns for worship. Care has to be taken, of course, that the glories of the gospel are not hidden by something extremely Jewish, which was more suited to the days of carnal ordinances and a worldly sanctuary. The veil of Moses can still cloud the beholding of the Saviour.

Our Lord and His disciples sang a hymn (Mt. 26:30). This was, most probably, the Jewish Hallel. Psalm 118, from which it is taken, however, is Messianic, and speaks of Christ. In singing the hymn, the Lord was no doubt claiming the fulfillment of its truth in Himself, and may have interpreted the scripture before they began to sing. In fact, the Lord had already done this in His teaching previous to their singing. The Messianic portion (vv. 22-27) contains four cardinal truths of the Christian faith. All these are revealed in that important chapter of Matthew 16, and all made clear by our Lord.

THE CHRIST

"The stone which the builders refused is become the head stone of the corner" (Ps. 118:22). The Lord used this word in Luke 20:17 to establish His Messiahship. So also with verse 26 of the psalm: "Blessed [is] He that cometh in the name of the Lord," which was shouted by the children of Jerusalem when our Lord rode into the city on the colt, the foal of an ass. Peter by divine revelation confessed our Lord to be that promised Messiah when he said, "Thou art the Christ [Messiah], the Son of the living God" (Mt. 16:16).

Three great truths were enshrined in the idea of the Messiah. First, He was to be the Son of David, the "rod out of the stem of Jesse" (Isa. 11:1). Secondly, He was to be the suffering Servant of Isaiah, "wounded for our transgressions...bruised for our iniquities" (Isa. 53:5). Thirdly, He was to be the triumphant Lord of all (Dan. 7:9-10, 13-14). This was the Messiah whom Israel's rulers rejected.

That the Son of God became Son of Man can never be accounted for on the principles of natural reason. How can that reason tell us how a virgin became a mother? It is a truth which must be embraced, understood only by divine revelation to the soul. That Jesus was the Christ was thus revealed to Peter and the other disciples, and so it is to all who believe.

THE CHURCH

The Church is not revealed in the Old Testament, but it lies hidden in such words from Psalm 118 as these: "The stone which the builders refused is become the head stone of the corner. This is the Lord's doing; it is marvellous in our eyes" (Ps. 118:22-23). To Israel

62

He was the "stone of stumbling, and a rock of offense" (1 Pet. 2:8). There is a tradition that in the building of Solomon's temple a great stone was first rejected which was later discovered to be the one for which they were looking to complete the great edifice.

In Matthew 16:18 is revelation of the second cardinal truth of the Christian faith—the Church. The Lord Jesus said, immediately following Peter's confession, that He was the Christ, "I will build My Church." It was this Church of which the Lord was to be "the head [stone] of the corner." This truth was taught by our Lord Himself in the parable of the husbandman (Mt. 21:42). The Church is our Lord's own building—a spiritual building built with living stones of regenerated men and women (1 Pet. 2:4-5), and He is that Living Stone, "disallowed indeed of men," from whom all these precious stones derive their new and heavenly life.

THE CROSS

"God is the Lord, which hath showed us light: bind the sacrifice with cords, even unto the horns of the altar" (Ps. 118:27). So reads the Jewish Hallel. This is fulfilled in the cross of the Lord Jesus, and is the third great truth revealed in Matthew 16, "From that time forth began Jesus to show unto His disciples how that He must go unto Jerusalem, and suffer many things of the elders and chief priests and scribes, and be killed, and be raised again the third day" (Mt. 16:21).

"God is the Lord, which hath showed us light." This He does to all who receive His grace. God shines into the heart of such "in the face of Jesus Christ" (2 Cor. 4:6), who is "the light of the world" (Jn. 8:12). That light shone on the day Paul was converted on the Damascus road. Paul could only say it was brighter than the noonday sun. In that light he saw light.

"Bind the sacrifice with cords...to...the altar." The sacrifices of the Old Testament's symbolic system were so bound before slaughter. In fulfillment of this, one finds in the Gospels several occasions when our Lord was bound. There were several of these bindings as He drew near to the cross, until at last He was bound to the cross itself, and then slain by crucifixion—a Roman death, the worst of all deaths, and a death connected with the curse. He was bound in turn by Annas, Caiaphas, Pilate, and Herod—but oh, rather, by the cords of divine love and that for our redemption.

Nothing took place in connection with His death but what was "according to the Scriptures," and therefore predetermined by God. In that death our Lord did not suffer merely as a martyr. That is true, but not the whole truth. Nor did He suffer only because He was a witness to truth. That also is true, but not the whole truth. The principal cause of His death was that He as Substitute took our place, and therefore was "made...sin for us" when He Himself knew no sin. Thus He died in our place.

THE COMING AGAIN

There was a second meaning to the words in the Hallel: "Blessed [is] He that cometh in the name of the Lord" (Ps. 118:26). It is a reference not only to His first coming, but also to His second coming. This verse looks forward to that blessed day when, through the Tribulation yet to come, all Israel shall repent of their transgression, sin, and iniquity, and shall say: "This is the day which the Lord hath made; we will rejoice and be glad in it" (Ps. 118:24).

This is the fourth great truth in Matthew 16: "For the Son of Man shall come in the glory of His Father with His angels; and then He shall reward every man according to his works" (Mt. 16:27). But He is to come first in the air to gather to Himself His redeemed ones before He comes to the earth to restore Israel. How our own hearts should speak now the language of the Hallel, for we who are His people shall surely say: "Blessed is He that cometh in the name of the Lord!" What a gathering and what rejoicing that will be!

> *Feast after feast thus comes and passes by;*
> *Yet passing, points to the glad feast above;*
> *Giving sweet foretaste of the festal joy,*
> *The Lamb's great bridal feast of bliss and love.*

> —HORATIUS BONAR

13

Christ as Lamb

Behold the Lamb of God.
JOHN 1:29

The Lamb of God is the central theme of the Holy Scriptures. All who wrote, inspired by the Spirit of God, pointed to Christ. That is what the whole Bible does. The Cross of Christ is the key to every epoch of human history. Jesus was the Lamb slain before the foundation of the world; He reigns today, and will reign throughout endless ages, as the enthroned Lamb in heaven. There are ten principal and chosen servants who set forth Christ in this touching title.

1. Abel: "Abel...brought of the firstlings of his flock" (Gen. 4:4). He, no doubt, had been taught by his parents the necessity of a blood sacrifice for sin. Cain, his elder brother, brought the fruit of his own toil, rejecting God's method, and was himself rejected. Abel followed divine directions, knowing that he was a sinful man, possessor of a fallen human nature, and brought a lamb, referred to as "a more excellent sacrifice" (Heb. 11:4). This spoke of *acceptance*.

2. Abraham: To bring Abraham into fellowship with all that was in His heart, God called him to sacrifice his only son Isaac. Here is the first mention of the actual word "lamb." As father and son went up mount Moriah, the place of sacrifice, Isaac asked: "My father...behold the fire and the wood: but where is the lamb for a

burnt offering?" After going through the test of faith to the uttermost, God called to Abraham: "Lay not thine hand upon the lad," and then, "Behold, behind him a ram caught in a thicket by his horns: and Abraham went and took the ram, and offered him up...in the stead of his son" (Gen. 22:7-13). This teaches *substitution.*

3. Moses and Israel: Exodus 12 is Israel's deliverance from Egypt. "They shall take to them every man a lamb" (v. 3). The blood of the lamb was to be sprinkled on the doorposts and on the lintel of their houses. God said, "When I see the blood, I will pass over you" (v. 13). Under the blood there was protection from the destroying angel. This spoke of *security.*

4. The Levites: These were ministers of the sanctuary, offering what became known as the Levitical offerings. The animals were to be "perfect to be accepted; there shall be no blemish therein" (Lev. 22:21). Only a perfect offering could make a perfect sacrifice so that it could meet all the challenges of sin. This spoke of *atonement.*

5. Isaiah: "He hath borne our griefs, and carried our sorrows...He was wounded for our transgressions, He was bruised for our iniquities: the chastisement of our peace was upon Him; and with His stripes we are healed" (53:4-5). The masculine pronoun suggests that He was to be a true Man, and in that manhood God's Lamb was to bear our sins in His own body. This pointed to His *sin-bearing.*

6. John the Baptist: "Behold the Lamb of God, which taketh away the sin of the world" (Jn. 1:29). This is the first mention of Christ as the Lamb in the New Testament and is an answer to Isaac's inquiry: "Where is the lamb?" (Gen. 22:7). In the fullness of time, the Son of God was manifested and introduced to the world by John as God's appointed Lamb of sacrifice. This announced the *removal of sin.*

7. Philip: An Ethiopian eunuch, Secretary of the Treasury, had come all the way to Jerusalem. He was obviously an earnest seeker after the true manner of worship. However, he found nothing in Jerusalem but a dead religious system, all the symbols of which had been done away with the coming of Christ. Philip was directed to meet this man on his way home and, running alongside his chariot and hearing him read from Isaiah 53, asked: "Understandest thou

what thou readest?" On being invited up into the chariot, Philip "began at the same Scripture and preached unto him Jesus." The Ethiopian was saved, baptized, and went on his way rejoicing. This declares the reality of *individual salvation.*

8. Peter: "Ye were not redeemed with corruptible things, as silver and gold...but with the precious blood of Christ, as of a lamb without blemish and without spot" (1 Pet. 1:18-19). That was the price paid for our redemption, but it was not a cash transaction. It was "blood of Christ" (Acts 20:28). This stated *the purchase price.*

9. John: John the apostle had been exiled by the Emperor Domitian to the island of Patmos. This place of limitation became the place of revelation. In a vision of a heavenly scene, John saw "in the midst of the throne...stood a Lamb as it had been slain" (Rev. 5:6). The Lamb who had been slain on earth was indeed risen from the dead and now enthroned in heaven. The Victim had become the Victor. This anticipates the *government* of the Lamb.

10. The Angel: "And...one of the seven angels...showed me that great city, the holy Jerusalem, descending out of heaven from God...and the city had no need of the sun, neither of the moon, to shine in it: for the glory of God did lighten it, and the Lamb is the light thereof" (Rev. 21:9, 10, 23). The Lamb shall forever be the Conveyor of all the blessing and glory of God. The glory of God shines through the Lamb so that there is no need for any created light (the sun), or reflected light (the moon), or manufactured light (the candle). This speaks of His eternal *glory.*

Behold the amazing sight!
The Saviour lifted high;
The Son of God, His soul's delight,
Expires in agony.

For whom, for whom, my heart,
Were all these sorrows borne?
Why did He feel that piercing smart,
And wear the crown of thorn?

67

For us in love He bled,
For us in anguish died;
'Twas love that bowed His sacred head
And pierced His precious side.

Behold, behold the amazing sight!
Nor trace His griefs alone,
But from the cross pursue our flight
To His triumphant throne.

—PHILIP DODDRIDGE

14

In Remembrance

This do in remembrance of Me.
1 CORINTHIANS 11:24

It is an astonishing thing that we who have been redeemed need a reminder of our Lord's death on the cross. Yet it is so! If we search our hearts and examine our ways, we shall find it is easy to forget. Our Lord, who knows well the weakness and treachery of our human hearts, has made provision for us to be constantly reminded. Thus He has established the memorial feast with this intent, "This do in remembrance of Me."

The Lord's things are sublime in their simplicity. This feast is so simple—"simple bread and simple wine, sweet memorials of our Lord." Faith alone can interpret these elements and in them catch the image of our beloved Saviour. Faith has learned the sound principle that natural things reflect the beauties and glories, even the sufferings of the Lord Jesus. It is seen in the elements on the table, the testimony of the true Bread and true Wine, and how He became food and drink for our souls.

It is most inspiring to read Church history and witness the many strange places where the saints have set up a table of sorts and used these simple memorials to remember their Lord. For instance, we find the Lord's people meeting in the catacombs of Rome, in the

Scottish moors, in concentration camps, in exiles' lonely prisons, on battlefields, in fact, in every kind of place.

A REQUESTED REMEMBRANCE

There is the Lord's own authority for observing this feast. It is no sentimental arrangement by some especially devoted believers. In these words of our text, which had been communicated to the Apostle Paul, the permanence of this service was established. It was instituted by the Lord Himself in Matthew 26:26-28. Acts 2:42 records the first occasion of believers' obedience to His command; and in Acts 20:7, we see that it became the general practice of the church to observe this on "the first day of the week."

The words, "this do" and "as oft as," contain the idea of repetition, that the feast is to be observed again and again. It is a request, as it were, written by our Lord's own pen. It is the decree of His own mouth, the fruit of His own omniscient mind, the perfection of His thought. All His instructions are surely designed by His wisdom and laid down by His grace. "I have received of the Lord," said Paul—which means a clear communication from the Lord. The observance, therefore, is never to be one of mere impulse or of natural inclination, but observed because the Lord has ordained that we should keep it.

A VISIBLE REMEMBRANCE

The form of the remembrance matches our weakness. We need to see something to aid our faith. We must handle things. It almost seems that pure faith is so feeble in most men that we need help through the physical senses. The Lord has provided for this need and given us these elements which can be seen and handled.

The history of God's dealings with man, especially in communicating profound truth, is full of visible and tangible objects for the senses to contemplate: the rainbow, the Passover meal, the booths at the Feast of Tabernacles, the rod of Aaron, the pot of manna, the stones of witness from the River Jordan, and hundreds more.

The bread and the wine are simply emblems—commemorative emblems. "This is My body"—not that the bread *is* His actual body,

70

but that it represents His body. "This cup is the new testament in My blood"—not that the cup *is* the testament, but that the wine in it is a token of the covenant. It is metaphorical language which all of us use every day. Is not our Lord's purpose clear as day? We are not to read mystical things into these simple emblems, and make them into something other than what they are. They picture Christ. They are models of His saving work. They are there with one design: to set forth Christ and proclaim His redeeming love.

A Strengthening Remembrance

This remembrance feast draws our hearts to God. While the elements on the table are only emblems, the feast is not a bare commemoration. We rise above the elements. We gaze at our Lord Himself, and it is on Him that our souls feed. The faith of the believer must look beyond the elements. All that our Lord is in Himself is the believer's portion.

Now that we are in Him, His wisdom is ours to guide; His power is ours to uphold; His faithfulness and truth are our shield and buckler; His Spirit is given us to teach, solace, and bless us; His righteousness is ours to make us walk uprightly; His heaven is ours to be our home. It is meditation on such blessed realities which is the strengthening portion of this feast.

A Personal Remembrance

"This do ye." Our remembrance of the Lord is more than a mere remembrance of the historical event of His dying. It is the remembrance that it was for each of us personally—for me, even me! He does not ask that we remember the date or even the place of His sacrifice, but that we remember Him. Our eyes must focus, not on the tree (on bits of wood supposedly from His cross, or bits of the napkin once wound around His head) but on the Lord Himself. In the same way, we are not to remember the Lord's Supper as a doctrine, or a precept, or an event; but we are to remember the Lord Himself. Our thought must not stray from Him. We are not to magnify a man who distributes the elements. We are not to magnify the ordinance.

We are not to make superstition out of this feast. We are to remember only the Lord Jesus.

A Spiritual Remembrance

This gathering to partake of the Lord's Supper is more than a ceremony. We are to come to it with spiritual affections. The spirit of the believer must be exercised; the heart must go out to Him. This means a sense of reverence and godly fear. We are to examine ourselves and so partake worthily; that is, we are to have regard to the true worth of the feast. We are not to come here complacently, or lightheartedly, or with outlandish clothes, but with deep searchings of heart and great appreciation of the wondrous Lord and Saviour, who is present in the midst. May God help us so to come.

According to Thy gracious Word,
In meek humility,
This would I do, O Christ my Lord;
I would remember Thee.

Thy body, broken for my sake,
My bread from heaven shall be;
Thy blood my peace, this cup I take,
And thus remember Thee.

When to the cross I turn my eyes,
And rest on Calvary,
O Lamb of God, my sacrifice,
I must remember Thee!
                    —James Montgomery

15
The Placarding of Christ

Before whose eyes Jesus Christ hath been
evidently set forth, crucified among you.
GALATIANS 3:1

Bishop Lightfoot has a good word in place of the phrase "evidently set forth." It is the word *placarded.* The Lord and His atoning work on the cross had been placarded before these Galatians. The message of His Person and work had been clearly demonstrated before them. But now they were falling back to the legalism of the Old Covenant. "O foolish Galatians!" What folly is this to leave Christ for Moses—the gospel for the law—justification by the righteousness of Christ which brings such solid comfort, for justification by the works of the law which could only bring their souls into bondage. The apostle was so astonished as to call them foolish or senseless.

THE EMPHASIS ON THE CROSS

Paul had placarded the cross before their eyes. We have often seen men carrying a large placard over their shoulders, hanging down front and back as a means of advertising. Paul had made "Christ crucified" as vivid and arresting as that to them.

The Old Covenant could never convey souls to heaven. It was too

73

weak to open those bright gates. It was too feeble to ascend the hill of the Lord. If we seek acceptance of God by Sinai's code, we must surely fail; it is folly to try it.

It is only the Lord Jesus and His atoning sacrifice on the cross which can make a way for us to heaven. On that cross He met every need. His finished work alone satisfies divine justice. He has given His life for mine. In Him—by Him—we clear the law's uttermost demand. Such is the value of the Saviour's cross, and its value was made clear by the apostle to these Galatians.

THE SCOPE OF THE CROSS

The cross of our Lord Jesus embraces and affects the whole universe of God:

1. *The cross is the center of a believer's life.* Believers stand fearless on the rock of a completed sacrifice: "It is finished!" Human redemption is secured, an accomplished fact. Every payment has been made in full. Every penalty has been endured. The cursed cup has been drained. Satan has been vanquished. Believers are free. So to the Galatians the apostle could write, "God forbid that I should glory, save in the cross of our Lord Jesus Christ," and, "I am crucified with Christ: nevertheless I live; yet not I, but Christ liveth in me" (Gal. 6:14; 2:20).

2. *The cross is the center of the corporate assembly.* The Lord has formed His Church by sovereign grace. He has planted it with His virtues, gifts, and graces. He waters it every moment. He has fenced it round with His almighty power. It is nourished with the refreshing doctrines of the gospel which are seasonably applied. It is impregnable against the forces of evil. Its faith, piety, and courage have spread to the ends of the earth. Because the cross is the center of the Church, "the gates of hell shall not prevail against it" (Mt. 16:18).

3. *The cross is the center of world history.* Everything beforehand moved toward the cross; everything since flows from that cross. The whole world was sunk in ruin and misery, given over to idolatry and superstition. No distinction is made for any person of any race: "All have sinned, and come short of the glory of God" (Rom. 3:23). "They

are all gone out of the way...there is none that doeth good, no, not one" (Rom. 3:12). But at the center of this ruined race, God has set forth a means whereby sin can be forgiven and guilt removed. That means is the cross of Christ which God has made a Mercy-seat.

4. *The cross is the center of the universe.* There is a state of disorder in the whole cosmos. But the regeneration of the whole is promised so that there is to be a new heaven and earth. Through the blood of the cross, God will "reconcile all things unto Himself... whether they be things in earth, or things in heaven" (Col. 1:20).

THE REACH OF THE CROSS

It gives assent to His holiness. The one grand purpose of the scheme of grace is to guard and secure God's holiness which is the very ground of His nature. Holiness was therefore manifest in our Lord's life on earth. His walk in our soiled path was as clean as when He moved on celestial pavement. His every act—every word—have but one feature, and that is one of absolute holiness. The cross reaches up to heaven and secures that holiness. It thus gives God righteous ground on which to forgive sinful men.

It also reaches down to the bottom of human degeneracy. Some may ask, "Can holiness revive the wasteland of nature upon which the blight and curse of God rests?" Only by means of the cross! The Lord Jesus alone can make a wretched sinner holy and fit for the presence of the holy God. The Saviour welcomed is holiness begun. The Saviour cherished is holiness advancing. The Saviour never absent is holiness complete. Holiness complete is fitness for heaven. Only through the cross can man rise to that heaven of heavens where God is, and live in God's holy presence without fear forever. O wondrous cross that can do that for us, and do it forever!

> *O perfect life of love!*
> *All, all is finished now;*
> *All that He left His throne above*
> *To do—for us below.*

And in His thorn-crowned head,
And in His sinless soul,
Our sins in all their guilt were laid,
That He might make us whole.

In perfect love He dies—
For me, He dies for me;
O all-atoning Sacrifice,
I cling by faith to Thee.

Yet work, O Lord, in me,
As Thou for me hast wrought;
And let my love the answer be
To grace Thy love has brought.

—HENRY WILLIAMS BAKER

16
Fellowship at the Feast

For we being many are one bread, and one body: for we are all
partakers of that one bread.
1 Corinthians 10:17

It is the blessed habit of the saints to especially remember our Lord at His own instituted remembrance feast. This ought to be our hearty resolve each Lord's Day. Nothing should be allowed to disturb these moments of quiet and sacred remembrance. Then let us put aside all worldly care, and all daily business, and all the griefs and sorrows of our earthly pilgrimage, gathering to Him and with His saints in this feast of love.

The Celebrants of the Past

It is pleasing to remember how many of all ages in the Christian Church have celebrated the remembrance feast and the sufferings and death of the Saviour in this, His appointed way. It has never been a crowded table; but it has never been a forsaken one. Many are now in heaven who were constant at His supper on earth, but now feast with Him in the banqueting halls of glory.

Many of these dear ones of ages past commemorated His sufferings and death at the risk of their lives. The mountaintops were not too cold; the moors and glens not too isolated; the caves of the

77

wilderness not too damp and drear for those noble souls who loved their Lord. They testified their devotion to Him at all hazards and under every hardship. They sat where the Belshazzars and Caesars of this world never sat, nor ever shall.

There was a good deal of zeal, warmth, and fervency in their devotion. Their excellent example stirs and excites our own love as we remember them. We cannot help but admire these saints of past days who cleaved to the Lord through grace, and with great purpose of heart kept the feast. They recognized His righteousness for their justification, His fullness for their every need, and His blood for their pardon and cleansing. They would not forget and therefore were resolved to keep the feast.

THE CELEBRANTS IN OUR OWN LAND

It is pleasing to remember, too, that there are many believers in our own land who come to this appointed ordinance. We who are of British stock have ancestors who once sat at "the table of devils," as in the case of the Druids. We read our history, and bow in shame as we read, that at one time our ancestors offered up human sacrifices, very popular in Britain at one time.

So we heartily rejoice that missionaries came and preached the gospel of God's saving grace so that converts among our forefathers set up the Lord's remembrance feast and spread the sacred elements in our land. Such dates are unknown; such places are unmarked; but the sweet influence of their faith and love has done its wonders and left behind a testimony of incalculable value among our people.

It is cause for praise that there are so many today, though few compared to the vast number of unbelievers, who count a day in His courts better than a thousand elsewhere, and delight to remember their Lord. They neither creep there by stealth, nor steal up, like Nicodemus, by night, but do so openly and publicly, and count it their joy and delight to thus meet the Lord at the remembrance table.

THE CELEBRANTS IN OTHER LANDS

It is also pleasing to remember that our Lord's sacrificial love in

His death is remembered on all continents and in practically all countries—in the great lands of China, Africa, India, and, maybe with the exception of a few Islamic lands, in all other places of the earth. I myself have been present at a thousand such gatherings in many lands, from the most southerly assembly in the world to almost the most northerly; from the most easterly in New Zealand to the most westerly in the Americas. Still they multiply, and the voice of adoring worship and praise never ceases in the earth.

Thus we are part of a great family of believers, "a multitude which no man can number," though we may meet in small local fellowships. These small groups, if they but thought of themselves, could easily feel discouraged or sad. But it is not so. The Lord is present in their midst, and they know they are loved by Him, that they are the gift of the Father to Him, that they are a possession purchased by His own blood. They are morsels together of the one great loaf.

There is an inseparable connection between our growth and increase in love and appreciation for the Saviour and the observance of this remembrance feast. Alas, we think of some who have grown cold in spiritual affections because of the neglect of it. There is nowhere else where we can be better established than in being engrossed and absorbed in remembering the love of Christ in His sacrifice for us.

There, too, we should see to it that, in coming, there is tender love for all the Lord's people. There should be no discord among the saints of God. It is a corporate fellowship of all who are saved by the Lord, and the loaf on the table testifies of that oneness. We are to exclude none who are born of God and who maintain a godly life. But we are to examine ourselves, too. We must put away all that is offensive to our Lord, then come and enjoy the feast with the Lord and all His redeemed ones.

O God, how wide Thy glory shines!
How high Thy wonders rise!
Known through the earth by thousand signs,
By thousands through the skies.

79

But when we view Thy strange design
To save rebellious worms,
Where vengeance and compassion join
In their divinest forms:

Now the full glories of the Lamb
Adorn the heavenly throne,
While saints on earth that know His name,
Their Lord and Saviour own.

—ISAAC WATTS

17
The Triumph of the Cross

And having spoiled principalities and powers, He made a show of
them openly, triumphing over them in it [the cross].
COLOSSIANS 2:15

Here is a matter which is often overlooked at the Lord's Supper. It
is the Lord's total destruction of the power of the enemy. Satan's
power through the sin of his rebellion lay in the setting up of a kingdom here on earth to forestall the kingdom which God intended to
establish through His beloved Son. This was a challenge on the part
of Satan to the dominion and authority of God, whose throne is in the
heavens and whose "kingdom ruleth over all" (Ps. 103:19).

God is infinite in His authority, and He prepared the course of the
universe for the well-being of all His creatures. God alone had
absolute right over all things within the circuit of heaven and earth.
In his challenge to this authority, Satan and his cohorts "kept not
their first estate" (Jude 6), which meant a rebellious break from the
place of God's assignment and an invasion into an area God had
reserved for man's dominion.

This rebellious spirit infected man when he listened to Satan's
voice in temptation and followed him. Man then came under the
power of Satan, becoming his slave to do his dark and devilish works.
This brought man into very great misery. He could never, in this con-

dition, be an essentially happy man, nor have any expectation of happiness in the eternal world to come. He had hewn out for himself broken cisterns that could hold no water.

It was necessary, therefore, that the Lord Himself come into this arena of earth, first to destroy the power of the devil, and thereafter to deliver men from under Satan's power. Through satanically controlled man, God's purposes for man's well-being had been disrupted. The Lord's advent, then, into this sphere of things had a double purpose which He Himself declared. The first would be the overthrow of Satan: "Now shall the prince of this world be cast out," and secondly the salvation of man: "I, if I be lifted up from the earth, will draw all men unto Me" (Jn. 12:31-32). These tremendous accomplishments could be worked out only by His entering into death. This is clear from John 12:33: "This He said, signifying what death He should die."

OUR LORD'S PERSONAL TRIUMPH

The Lord had a personal score to settle with Satan. There would have been little point in saving man if He had left the power of Satan over man intact. That power first had to be broken if man was to be saved and set free. As our Lord went to the cross, therefore, with respect to His contact with Satan, He went forward as a conqueror. In entering into death, He was entering into the citadel, the stronghold of Satan. Death was his mighty fortress, and the Lord entered that fortress that "through death He might destroy him that had the power of death, that is, the devil" (Heb. 2:14). And this He did. He utterly disarmed Satan of his power, and "having spoiled principalities and powers, He made a show of them openly, triumphing over them in it." Satan was caught in a classic trap set by divine wisdom.

God had allowed Satan power over man, since man had followed that prince of evil. It was part of the punishment of sin to be brought under Satan's power. Because God sent forth His Son into our humanity, Satan supposed he had that same power over the Son of God, now that He had become Son of Man. This thought must have been strengthened in Satan's mind when he saw the Lord reduced to

82

physical weakness on the cross.

But Satan had no power at all over Christ as the Son of Man. Therefore, in attacking our Lord, Satan fell into the trap and met the almighty power of the One who was the God-Man. Satan was therefore spoiled so that he could never again rise to challenge the Lord Jesus. The victory of the cross was final and complete as far as our Lord was concerned. It was His personal triumph.

OUR LORD'S TRIUMPH ON OUR BEHALF

"And deliver them who through fear of death were all their lifetime subject to bondage" (Heb. 2:15). The devil had power over men. He derived that power from man's surrender to him when presented with temptation's snare. Man became Satan's vassal. The power of Satan over man lay in sin, and the strength of sin was the law, which condemned sin and so condoned Satan's power over sinful man. But in the cross three things were effected by our Lord.

First, God was able to forgive sins on the basis of righteous justice. It provided a way whereby God is "just, and the justifier of him which believeth in Jesus." By that cross we are redeemed, ransomed, bought with a price, reconciled to God, adopted through grace, because our Lord made a full, perfect, and sufficient sacrifice, a satisfaction for the sins of the whole world. All the punishment which sin incurred was borne by the Lord, so that man could be "forgiven...all trespasses" (Col. 2:13). The sin question was settled at the cross once and for all. Coming to Him, a sinner receives the everlasting benefits of pardon and forgiveness and everlasting life.

Secondly, there was the "blotting out [of] the handwriting of ordinances that was against us...nailing it to His cross" (Col. 2:14). That means that all indictments of law were answered and fulfilled on our behalf. The law was made honorable and, being satisfied with payment made in full, blotted out the handwriting of ordinances which was against us.

Thirdly, and importantly, "having spoiled principalities and powers [on our behalf also], He made a show of them openly, triumphing over them in it" (Col. 2:15). The Lord Jesus, in His cross, deprived all the hosts of hell of their power over believers, and has shown them off to believers as defeated foes. This is to the shame of such evil powers and to the honor of the Son of God. The cross provides certainty of complete and permanent triumph on our behalf, and thus enables believers to live in the good of that victory. The keys of death are now in our Lord's hands and under His control. He is Lord even over the devils and the damned.

Thus, being made partakers of our Lord's life and victory, every believer should live free from Satan's power, and go forth with freedom to do the Father's will in the strength of our Lord's risen and triumphant life. There need be no defeat ever.

Yet even in our moments of weakness, our Lord triumphs. If we call upon Him in the moment of danger, we find that "The name of the Lord is a strong tower: the righteous runneth into it, and is safe" (Prov. 18:10).

> *Sunk in ruin, sin, and misery,*
> *Bound by Satan's captive chain,*
> *Guided by his artful treachery,*
> *Hurrying on to endless pain,*
> *My Redeemer, my Redeemer,*
> *Plucked me as a brand from hell.*
>
> *Mine by covenant, mine forever,*
> *Mine by oath, and mine by blood;*
> *Mine, nor time the bond shall sever,*
> *Mine as an unchanging God.*
> *My Redeemer, my Redeemer,*
> *Oh, how sweet to call Thee mine!*

—AUTHOR UNKNOWN

18

Between Resurrection & Ascension

To whom also He showed Himself alive after His passion by many
infallible proofs, being seen of them forty days.

ACTS 1:3

The Lord's death and resurrection, when viewed in connection with the Old Testament dispensation, summed it up and brought it to an end. The Lord remained on earth for forty days after His resurrection to prepare His disciples for the new age of grace. During these days there were appearances and disappearances. The appearances were necessary in order to prove again and again that He was indeed risen from the dead. The disappearances were necessary in order to school His disciples to live by faith and not by sight since His bodily presence was soon to be taken away. In this period there were seven important openings.

THE OPENING OF THE TOMB

We are told in Mark 16:1 that certain women brought sweet spices to anoint the body of the Lord and found the huge stone already rolled away from the door of the tomb. There had been an earthquake (Mt. 28:2), and an angel from heaven had moved it. The guards who were on duty became "as dead men." No one saw Jesus come out of the tomb. The stone was not rolled away to let Jesus out—He was

85

already out—but to let the disciples in that they might see the evidence that He had risen. The Lord did not have to struggle out of clothes to rise. In quiet and calm control, He rose without disturbing the grave clothes. The Lord opened the door of death and rose triumphant over it.

THE OPENING OF THE HEAVENS

Mark 16:19 tells us, "He was received up into heaven." "Thou hast ascended on high" (Ps. 68:18) means that He did so by His own inherent power, and was given a royal welcome. The language of the psalm is that of a military triumph—the Lord having defeated all the hierarchy of hell and fully accomplished man's redemption. Thus in Psalm 24 we see heaven opening its gates to receive Him. "Lift up your heads, O ye gates; and be ye lift up, ye everlasting doors; and the King of glory shall come in. Who is this King of glory? The Lord strong and mighty, the Lord mighty in battle." He opened those gates, and open they remain until the last of His believing people pass through to sit with Him in everlasting glory.

THE OPENING OF THE EYES

"And their eyes were opened" (Lk. 24:31), so that "they knew Him." The prophets had declared that He would do this (Isa. 35:5). The first reference of this scripture may have been to physical eyes. Few of such eyes were opened, but millions of spiritual eyes have been opened since, and all such now know the Lord. All His followers need this touch of His risen life. We read of the two going to Emmaus that "their eyes were holden that they should not know Him" (Lk. 24:16); that Mary in the garden was actually standing near Him yet "knew not that it was Jesus"; that the disciples who had gone back fishing "knew not that it was Jesus" standing on the seashore. All needed their eyes opened that they might know Him in resurrection life.

THE OPENING OF THE FUTURE

"Verily, verily, I say unto thee," said the Lord to Peter, "When thou

86

wast young, thou girdest thyself, and walkedst whither thou wouldst: but when thou shalt be old, thou shalt stretch forth thy hands, and another shall gird thee, and carry thee whither thou wouldst not. This spake He, signifying by what death he should glorify God" (Jn. 21:18-19). The Lord in these words told Peter two things. First, he would live to be an old man and, secondly, by which exit door he would depart out of this world. When Peter turned and saw John following, he asked the Lord, "What shall this man do?" The Lord answered, in effect, that that was not Peter's business. John's future, too, was in the hands of the Lord. So are all our futures.

THE OPENING OF THE SCRIPTURES

"Did not our heart burn within us...while He opened to us the Scriptures?" (Lk. 24:32). The two on the way to Emmaus were in the depths of despondency. The cross had blasted their hopes of an immediate earthly kingdom. But the Lord appeared to them, and though they did not recognize Him, He walked with them. In that walk He opened up a new ministry of finding Christ in all the ·Scriptures. "Beginning at Moses and all the prophets, He expounded unto them in all the Scriptures the things concerning Himself." As He did so, their heart burned within them. They were lifted out of their despair. The opening of the Scriptures set their hearts aflame.

THE OPENING OF THEIR UNDERSTANDING

"Then opened He their understanding, that they might understand the Scriptures" (Lk. 24:45). Education is not the key to such understanding, though no one would despise it. Many of the best teachers of the Word of God have had little in the way of formal education. Worldly philosophers have no clue to such understanding. But humble believers with very little education have often gone down into the depths of the Word and come up with hands laden with jewels of divine truth.

THE OPENING OF THE WORLD

"And they went forth, and preached everywhere, the Lord work-

87

ing with them" (Mk. 16:20). These disciples had been hidden behind closed doors, eating and drinking. When the risen Lord came into their midst, He upbraided them, then sent them out into all the world. "Go ye into all the world and preach the gospel to every creature." The whole world was their parish. Oiled wheels run freely. And how prompt and ready should we all be to witness for the Lord to all men everywhere, especially when endued with power from on high. "Here am I, send me" (Isa. 6:8), was Isaiah's prompt reply.

> *I know that my Redeemer lives:*
> *What comfort this sweet sentence gives!*
> *He lives, He lives, who once was dead;*
> *He lives my everlasting Head.*
>
> *He lives, triumphant from the grave;*
> *He lives, eternally to save;*
> *He lives, all glorious in the sky;*
> *He lives, exalted there on high.*
>
> *He lives, my mansion to prepare;*
> *And He will bring me safely there;*
> *He lives, all glory to His Name!*
> *Jesus, unchangeably the same!*

—SAMUEL MEDLEY

19

The Kiss

Judas...kissed Him.
MATTHEW 26:47-49

This woman...hath not ceased to kiss My feet.
LUKE 7:45

Let Him kiss me with the kisses of His mouth.
SONG OF SOLOMON 1:2

A kiss has many meanings in Scripture. Joseph kissed all his brethren as a token of reconciliation (Gen. 45:15). Orpah kissed Naomi, but returned to her paganism in Moab, while Ruth "clave" to her mother-in-law (Ruth 1:14). David kissed Jonathan in their final farewell—a kiss of friendship (1 Sam. 20:41). The father of the prodigal son "fell on his neck and kissed him" on the son's return (Lk. 15:20). In the Church, Paul admonished believers to "greet ye one another with an holy kiss" (1 Cor. 16:20).

As to the latter, we must remember that as in the Far East today, men and women sat separately, and greeted one another separately, so that this kiss was no doubt confined to members of the same gender. It was a "kiss of charity" (1 Pet. 5:14) and had the same effect as a love feast in India—it abolished all social distinctions and any spirit of discrimination and partiality among the Lord's people.

THE KISS OF JUDAS

"Now he that betrayed Him gave them a sign, saying, Whomsoever I shall kiss, that same is He: hold Him fast. And forthwith he came to Jesus, and said, Hail, Master—and kissed Him" (Mt. 26:48-49). The word used here means *fervently*. This betrayal kiss was more demonstrative than the ordinary kiss of a formal greeting. Never in all the years of His association with the intimate band of disciples did Judas ever call Jesus, "Lord"! His discipleship had been play acting, the very essence of hypocrisy.

Judas had privileges few men ever had. He companied with our Lord and belonged to a band of men who were to attend Him in His impeccable walk on earth, to hear His purpose to undergo the uttermost of God's wrath and to drink the very dregs of anguish for man's redemption. He must have seen the signs of coming distress on our Lord's face as He approached the mysterious depths of His substitutionary sacrifice and the shameful cross.

Was Judas so perverse and hardened that he never at any time read the language of the Saviour's heart, interpreted His incessant prayers, the meaning of His mighty pleadings, the appeal of His outstretched hands? Yet Judas betrayed Him, and did so with the sweetest symbol of love. It is the only time we read of anyone kissing the Saviour's face, and it was with the filthy lips of this betrayer, whose very name has become a symbol of infamy.

THE KISSES OF LOVE BY A WOMAN

"Seest thou this woman?" said our Lord in a gentle but stinging rebuke to Simon the Pharisee, who had given Him no water to wash His feet, no kiss of greeting, no oil for His refreshing. "This woman since the time I came in hath not ceased to kiss My feet" (Lk. 7:45). It is not likely that the woman was Mary Magdalene, nor Mary of Bethany, though the latter did much the same in anointing the Lord. This woman was a woman of sin, and our Lord's forgiveness had brought forth this act of pure devotion. She had tasted that the Lord is gracious and expressed her love of Him in this lowly and loving act of covering His feet with her kisses, the beautiful feet of the One who brought news from a very far country.

This act of complete devotion brought from the Saviour an assurance to Simon of her sins forgiven, "Her sins, which are many, are forgiven: for she loved much" (v. 47). That word must have dropped in her guilt-ridden soul like "sweet smelling myrrh" and carried its own blessing and refreshing. Her kisses upon His feet expressed her deep sense of unworthiness, but also demonstrated a soul now filled with love of Him. She had no doubt heard His public utterances of good news and sought Him out. What passion of affection! How much her heart was set on God's beloved Son! How desirous she was of His word of forgiveness! Her kisses on His feet were out of the abundance of her heart and must have given a great deal of satisfaction to our Lord.

THE KISS DESIRED BY HIS BRIDE

"Let Him kiss me with the kisses of His mouth" (Song of Sol. 1:2). This book is "the song of songs"—that is, unexcelled by any other song; and unsurpassed by any other song, whether of divine or human origin. There is no adequate interpretation of this song except that which relates it to the love union between Christ and His people. He is the Bridegroom-lover; she the bride.

Here she desires a new discovery of His affection, a new touch of His love upon her life. Here the kiss has spiritual significance since in this book we are in the realm of heavenly things. She seeks something more intimate and real than mere form and ceremony. Rather, she seeks "the kisses of His mouth." The love of Christ is a believer's true desire. It is the purest desire of the human soul to long after some special demonstration of it, which has the effect of raising our affections toward Him.

To have such a touch of His love on our lives is a believer's heaven on earth, and the beginning of glory. A believer prefers this to the most excellent things of earth. It is a surprising and astonishing grace that the blessed Lord of glory would stoop to kiss such wretches as we are, and to receive us into His loving embrace.

When we gather to Him, we should do so with this fond desire. True, we are here at the remembrance feast to express our devotion to Him, but the best incentive to do that will be to feel His touch of love upon our own lives. It would not be inappropriate at all to come to this feast of love with this desire: "Let Him kiss me with the kisses of His mouth."

Longing for the Bride, Lord Jesus,
Of Thy heart,
To be with Thee in the glory,
Where Thou art:
Love so groundless, grace so boundless,
Wins my heart.

When Thy blood-bought Church, Lord Jesus,
Is complete;
When each soul is safely landed
At Thy feet;
What a story in the glory
She'll repeat!

Then Thy Church will be, Lord Jesus,
The display
Of Thy richest grace and kindness
In that day;
Marking pages, wondrous stages,
O'er earth's way.

—MISS C. A. WELLESLEY

20
The Drink Offering

The drink offering thereof shall be of wine.
LEVITICUS 23:13

Wine, which cheereth God and man.
JUDGES 9:13

On most occasions in the tabernacle ceremonies of the Old Testament, wine was outpoured and, as a drink offering, completed the worship. A cup was there, and in the cup a wine offering. The revealing rays of the Spirit make faith to fly from this to the last paschal feast which our Lord interrupted to inaugurate His own remembrance feast. It was here that our Lord took a cup full of the juice of the vine, uplifted His thanks, then gave the cup to His little flock, saying, "This is My blood of the new testament, which is shed for many for the remission of sins" (Mt. 26:28).

Thus wine is a gospel sign. It takes its place among the holiest of symbols. "This is My blood!" And this symbol is the key which opens to us the treasure of the drink offering of old. It is one of the choicest emblems of redeeming grace.

The blood which streamed from the Man on Calvary's cross is of infinite and exceeding preciousness. It speaks first of our Lord's true manhood. Jesus had blood, or else He could not have been man.

Without blood, He could not have been a true kinsman of our race. And He must be true man if He would be man's Surety.

But let us never forget that He assumes this manhood without ceasing to be God. His blood, symbol of life, is man's blood, yet the blood flows through the veins of One who is God. This is a most profound mystery to us mortal men, and we can never fathom the uniqueness of the Person of the Lord Jesus Christ.

We now go forward to Calvary's cross to see our Lord pouring forth His blood. Until this precious blood flows, there is no remission of sin (Heb. 9:22). But our Lord does not withhold His blood. It begins to fall in circumcision when He is eight days old, later in Gethsemane's garden, then when scourged, again when He is crowned with thorns; finally, it is fully outpoured at the cross. His brow, His hands, His feet, His side, His heart—all weep blood. This is the sure proof that atonement has been made. Without the shedding of blood no sin could be forgiven—no atonement made. But in the shedding of His most precious blood, our Lord paid a full redemption price for us, and made salvation possible to all men everywhere.

In Scripture, wine also speaks of joy. "Wine, which cheereth God and man." Thus blood and joy are joined together. And that joy is marvelous.

JOY TO GOD

From all eternity, God has desired a race of exultant souls with Him in heaven. That was the divine intention. But a mighty barrier interposed. Sin came between God and man and separated them. How, then, could this barrier be removed? Sin had dug a very deep abyss for man. How could sin-fettered souls and sin-defiled hearts enter God's holy heaven? Jesus came and took away the barrier, and God now sees believers complete in Him. The great sacrifice on the cross cleared the way for God by grace to fulfill His plans.

JOY TO ANGELS

Angels, too, yearned that fallen man be saved. When a sinful man becomes saved, we read that there is a mighty outburst of celestial joy among the angels of heaven (Lk. 15:10). If this is so over one sinner that repents, what loud praises there must be over the whole multitude of the redeemed! All this happy rejoicing among the angels of heaven is made possible through the sacrificial death of the Lord Jesus. The angels of heaven know well that if all of them together had consented to die, such corporate death could not have saved a single sinner. They know who He was who died on Calvary's cross, and thus they cry: "Worthy is the Lamb that was slain." He is the supreme delight of the angels.

JOY TO MEN

Peter speaks of this joy to men as "unspeakable" (1 Pet. 1:8), that is, something beyond adequate expression. Gratitude can only utter its thanks in feeble praise and joyful song. Through the outpouring of this precious blood by the Son of God, the great Creator God (the sovereign Ruler over all things) becomes the portion of believers. He becomes their Father and their God, and they have access to His smile and favor. The heart of man can know no happier throb than to be able to look up into the face of the living God, the blessed and only Potentate, and say, "Father!"

Men search for happiness in vain if they seek it not in Christ the Lord. God can never give joy to any man apart from faith in His beloved Son—for there is no other channel of conveyance for that joy except through His Son and the sacrifice He made for sin. The blood of the Lord Jesus, in symbol, is in this cup. Here, in the wine which the cup contains, is the emblem of His most precious blood, and in the pouring out of that blood you can read all the heart of God, the travail and passion of His great love for us. Let our souls rise in heavenly joy and grateful praise to Him who loved us, and gave Himself for us. May we adore Him forever!

> *Rejoice and be glad!*
> *The Redeemer has come!*
> *Go look on His cradle,*
> *His cross and His tomb.*

95

Chorus:
    Sound His praises! Tell the story
    Of Him who was slain!
    Sound His praises! Tell with gladness
    He liveth again!

Rejoice and be glad!
Now the pardon is free!
The Just for the unjust
Has died on the tree.

Rejoice and be glad!
For the Lamb that was slain
O'er death is triumphant,
And liveth again.

—HORATIUS BONAR

21
Worshipers in the Old Testament

Praise waiteth for Thee, O God, in Sion.
PSALM 65:1

It is very instructive to note in the Scriptures the engagements or circumstances which brought forth worship from believing men or women. The attractiveness of divine worship, and the variety of events which stirred that worship are both inspiring and informative.

ABRAHAM OFFERING ISAAC

"And Abraham said unto his young men, Abide ye here with the ass; and I and the lad will go yonder and worship" (Gen. 22:5). The Lord God was taking Abraham into His own heart to know the fellowship of His sufferings. God's passion was derived from the sacrifice He was to make of His own beloved Son. Abraham therefore was asked for the sacrifice of his only son, and in responding to this, Abraham performed one of the most extraordinary acts of obedience that was ever known from the foundation of the world. The most amazing thing in this record—and there are things of the heart over which the Divine Recorder has cast a veil—is that Abraham calls this tremendous sacrifice an act of worship: "I and the lad will go yonder and worship." Abraham esteemed God *worthy* of the surrender of his dearest possession.

97

ELIEZER FINDING A BRIDE

"And the man [Eliezer] bowed down his head, and worshiped the Lord" (Gen. 24:26). Abraham had sent his faithful servant to find a bride for his beloved son, Isaac. It was a long, arduous journey through hundreds of miles of desert, since the bride was to come from Abraham's native land, from among his own kindred. It is a lovely picture of God sending His Spirit to choose out and bring home a bride for Christ, that bride being the great company of the redeemed (Rev. 21:9). The faithful servant was divinely led to Rebekah, who was endowed even before she received the message concerning Isaac, but who, on hearing the testimony, fully responded, and left all that was represented by her relatives to go on that long journey, at the end of which she would meet her Isaac. The point to remember is that the faithful servant was so led by God—"I being in the way, the Lord led me" (Gen. 24:27)—that "he bowed...his head, and worshiped the Lord" for such unerring guidance.

ISRAEL HEARING OF GOD'S CONCERN FOR THEM

"And the people believed: and when they heard that the Lord had visited the children of Israel, and that He had looked upon their affliction, then they bowed their heads and worshiped" (Ex. 4:31). Moses, after being on the mount with God, brought them the good news of God's visitation and His purpose to deliver them. It was a word of salvation. They were no longer to be vassals of a cruel taskmaster, but subjects of the Lord's own kingdom, and forged into a people for His using. The presence of Israel in Egypt was due to failure, but God was to redeem them from all the consequences of that failure and bring them out. When the people heard from Moses that God was to be the God of their salvation and that He would "come down to deliver"—a word which pointed forward to the incarnation of the Son of God—"they bowed their heads and worshiped."

JOSHUA'S ENTRANCE INTO THE PROMISED LAND

"Art Thou for us, or for our adversaries? And He said, Nay; but as captain of the host of the Lord am I now come. And Joshua fell on his face to the earth, and did worship" (Josh. 5:13-14). Moses had laid down his leadership. Though he had strong and holy desires to enter the land, yet God had forbidden it. In a public demonstration of anger he had dishonored God, and since he personified the law, which he and all others had broken, it was not possible for him to lead Israel into the Lord's inheritance. Joshua (meaning *Saviour*) fittingly took over. Before any battle was joined to gain possession, he was confronted by One who turned out to be a divine personage. Not knowing at first who He was, Joshua challenged His presence, but when the Lord explained that He had come to take over as Captain in order to ensure victory in their battles and the right of possession, Joshua "fell on his face to the earth, and did worship."

GIDEON HEARING GOD'S WORD THROUGH A DREAM

"And it was so, when Gideon heard the telling of the dream, and the interpretation thereof, that he worshiped" (Judg. 7:15). Israel was now confronted with a Midianite threat which had developed because of their own lapse back into idolatry. Gideon, called by God, had broken down the images and idols of vanity and cut down the groves. No deliverance could possibly come through such religious falsity. But God had come through in Gideon. To strengthen his confidence against such an enemy power, the Lord sent him and his servant into the camp of the Midianites. There they heard a man telling a dream about a cake of barley bread tumbling into the camp and wrecking it. Whereupon his fellow interpreted the barley cake as "nothing else save the sword of Gideon." This gave Gideon the assurance of victory, inspired courage, and drew forth worship.

SAMUEL IN HIS INFANCY

"And he worshiped the Lord there" (1 Sam. 1:28). In the background there is a husband with two wives, Peninnah and Hannah. Peninnah was fruitful after the flesh, but Hannah was barren. Peninnah is spoken of as Hannah's "adversary," who by her ridicule caused her to "fret" so that Hannah was brought into "bitterness of

99

soul." Hannah means "grace" and grace was not content with barren love. But the age was one of spiritual declension and Hannah was exercised for a child, not to glory in the flesh, nor for her own pleasure, but that the Lord might have an instrument for His using. In a most noble passage, which manifests Hannah's whole and complete consecration, she says: "For this child I prayed; and the Lord hath given me my petition which I asked of Him: therefore also I have lent him to the Lord; as long as he liveth he shall be lent to the Lord." That was Hannah. Then follows, "And he [not she][1] worshiped the Lord there"—which means even the heart of old Eli was moved to worship the Lord.

A CONGREGATION FOR THE OFFERING

"And David said to all the congregation, Now bless the Lord your God. And all the congregation blessed the Lord God of their fathers, and bowed down their heads, and worshiped the Lord" (1 Chron. 29:20). David had been denied the building of God's house in favor of his son, Solomon. This may have been a blow to David's desires, since the house was connected with the glory of God, and in it God's glory would be manifested. David, however, did not pout at God's denial, but with great affection for the testimony, gathered the materials for the building, himself contributing a great deal of the costliest and weightiest of metals—gold and silver. Following David's noble example, the whole congregation "offered willingly," and after David had led them in thanksgiving, they spontaneously "bowed their heads, and worshiped the Lord."

A REMNANT AT THE READING OF GOD'S WORD

"And Ezra the priest brought the law…And he read therein…from the morning until midday, before the men and the women, and those that could understand; and the ears of all the people were attentive unto the book of the law…And Ezra blessed the Lord, the great God. And all the people…bowed their heads, and worshiped the Lord with

1. Some ancient versions read, "They worshiped the Lord there."

their faces to the ground" (Neh. 8:2-3, 6). Here we see how the Word of God quickens the soul and energizes it to worship. Ezra's day was toward the end of that dispensation. Only a remnant had returned from the Babylonian captivity and did so with purpose of heart to raise again the Lord's testimony in a new temple. Ezra's strategy to inspire them to do this was to read the living Word of God to them, and the effect was so great that "they bowed their heads, and worshiped the Lord with their faces to the ground."

<h3 style="text-align:center">JOB IN THE LOSS OF ALL THINGS</h3>

"Then Job arose, and rent his mantle, and shaved his head, and fell down upon the ground, and worshiped" (Job 1:20). Satan had challenged God's attestation of Job's good character. His allegation was that self-interest lay behind the allegiance. The trial of Job was therefore consented to by the Lord, and the trial turned to the honor of Job.

At a second challenge, to meet Satan's taunt that Job's continued loyalty was because nothing had touched the man himself, God permitted Satan to afflict Job's body, which he did with "sore boils." Added to this was the loss of respect, through his friends misinterpreting his sufferings, and also through the loss of his wife's fellowship in faith. Job, however, had such love towards God's holy name, and such moderation with respect to his losses and crosses, and was of such fine resolution still to think well of God, that he "fell down upon the ground, and worshiped."

These are all acts of worship which God has regarded as worthy of permanent record in His Scriptures.

Father, Thy name our souls would bless,
As children taught by grace,
Lift up our hearts in righteousness
And joy before Thy face.

Sweet is the confidence Thou giv'st,
Though high above our praise,
Our hearts resort to where Thou liv'st
In heaven's unclouded rays.

O Holy Father, keep us here
In that blest name of love,
Walking before Thee without fear
Till all be joy above.

—J. N. DARBY

22
Worshipers in the New Testament

And [they] worshiped Him that liveth for ever and ever.
REVELATION 5:14

There is no proper ground of worship except that the object of worship have divine attributes. It is because the Lord Jesus is a divine person, the Second Person of the Triune God and "God manifest in the flesh," that He is given and receives worship. His incarnation is set forth in Scripture with crystal clearness and preeminence, because if He is not truly man then His history is a myth; and if He be not God, to worship Him is idolatry. For Him to receive worship is a robbery of that glory which alone is due to God. That is why His deity and His proper manhood are so clearly displayed in the Scriptures, why we find both men and angels giving Him worship, and we find Him receiving that worship.

THE WISE MEN AT THE BIRTH OF CHRIST

"Now when Jesus was born in Bethlehem of Judea in the days of Herod the king, behold, there came wise men from the east to Jerusalem, saying, Where is He that is born King of the Jews?" (Mt. 2:1-2) These wise men had doubtless been given divine revelation concerning the exalted person who had become incarnate. It is quite probable that they came from the land where Daniel had been president for so many long years, and that they had received the light of revelation through his inspired writings. The wise men were Gentiles, and were led over a trackless wilderness by the Spirit of God, to the very house where the Lord was to be found.[1] They had come to Bethlehem, as Micah had declared that this little village would be His birthplace (Micah 5:2). "And when they were come into the house, they...worshiped Him." The revelation of Him through the Divine Word ever issues in worship before Him.

MARINERS AT THE STILLING OF THE SEA

"Then they that were in the ship came and worshiped Him, saying, Of a truth Thou art the Son of God" (Mt. 14:33). The Lord had sent His disciples on this journey, so they were moving in His will and by His direction. Nevertheless, they were brought into an extremely difficult circumstance with high waves tossing the ship and a contrary wind that made progress impossible. It became dark, and through that darkness they saw what appeared to them an apparition or phantom.

Anything in that mysterious realm frightens mortal men. It was not a ghost but, seeing they thought it was, it terrified them. It happened to be the Lord Himself, mastering all elements in His approach to them, and perhaps coming to them in this extraordinary way because He could not get through to them in the ordinary. His assuring word was: "Be of good cheer; it is I; be not afraid." Jesus mildly rebuked Peter for his "little faith." In attempting to walk on the water, Peter took his eyes off the Lord and, putting them on surrounding waves, began to sink. As the storm immediately ceased by our Lord's direct command, they that were in the ship, seeing His absolute control over the elements, "worshiped Him."

A WOMAN AT THE HEALING OF HER DAUGHTER

"Then came she and worshiped Him, saying, Lord, help me" (Mt.

---

1. He being now between one and two years of age, the family had moved into a more permanent dwelling.

15:25). She was a woman of Canaan, a Syrophenician, who first addressed the Lord as "Thou Son of David." Had He opened His mouth to her as the Son of David, this would have spelled out her doom because of the decree in Zechariah 14:21. After further entreaty, He seemed to raise barrier after barrier, seemingly impossible for any to overcome. But this woman's faith leaped over every hurdle. As one who had no goodness to plead and no claim to advance, yet acknowledging Him as Lord of all, "she came and worshiped Him." That wonderful worshipful spirit was to take her through every testing until the Lord said, "O woman, great is thy faith: be it unto thee even as thou wilt."

THE WOMEN ON RESURRECTION MORN

"And as they went to tell His disciples, behold, Jesus met them, saying, All hail. And they came and held Him by the feet, and worshiped Him" (Mt. 28:9). The two Marys had been to the graveyard looking for a Christ whom they assumed to be still in the tomb. But they were met by angels who assured them, "He is not here: for He is risen, as He said" (v. 6). They were then instructed to "go quickly, and tell His disciples that He is risen from the dead." Immediately they ran to do so. How glad they must have been! With what excitement they must have run! But now, as they ran, the Lord Jesus met them in the way, and greeted them in the power of His resurrection life. Knowing Him now as the risen Lord, "They...held Him by the feet, and worshiped Him."

THE DISCIPLES IN VIEW OF BETHANY

"And they worshiped Him, and returned to Jerusalem with great joy" (Lk. 24:52). The last thing the risen Lord did before His ascension was to lead His disciples until they were opposite Bethany. He brought Bethany into view and, in this, seemed to be giving them a picture of what He intended His Church to be. There was no elaborate structure over there, but a home He loved to visit and with whose members He had the most tender association. There were, in that house, Mary, who expressed perfect love; Martha, who expressed

105

faithful service; and Lazarus, who expressed resurrection life. These were to be the essential elements in every true believer and the three phases of testimony which were to be the mark of their new life in Him. When Bethany therefore came into view, "He lifted up His hands, and blessed them. And...was parted from them, and carried up into heaven." With that completion of their preparation for the future, and the vision of the Church He was to build, "they worshiped Him."

THE BLIND MAN ON RECEIVING HIS SIGHT

"And he said, Lord, I believe. And he worshiped Him" (Jn. 9:38). This was a man blind from birth, so representative of the spiritual condition of all men. The Lord did one thing for this man and that one thing transformed his whole life. It gave him the faculty of sight which up to this time he did not have, and on being restored, he no longer needed to beg. The pharisaical rulers of Jewry were envious and inflamed because their man-made traditions had been breached by our Lord restoring a man's sight on the Sabbath day. When they examined the man, they heard a testimony of simple fact, though the man as yet did not know who had healed him. "Whether he be a sinner or no, I know not: one thing I know, that, whereas I was blind, now I see."

For presuming to have more spiritual wisdom than they, which now he did have, "they cast him out" (Jn. 9:34). The synagogue which had not been able to restore his sight through many long years, now excommunicated the man because another had done what they could not do. The Lord, however, did not leave the restored one in any perplexity. Jesus found him, and said to him, "Dost thou believe on the Son of God? He answered and said, Who is He, Lord, that I might believe on Him? And Jesus said unto Him, Thou hast both seen Him, and it is He that talketh with thee. And he said, Lord, I believe. And he worshiped Him."

THE REDEEMED IN HEAVEN

"And the four and twenty elders fell down and worshiped Him that

106

liveth for ever and ever" (Rev. 5:14). The scene is a heavenly one—
"a door was opened in heaven" (4:1). John wept at man's inability to
open the book of title deeds that was in the hands of the Lord God
sitting on the throne of haven. But he was commanded to "weep not"
because "the Lion of the tribe of Judah, the Root of David [David's
Lord], hath prevailed to open the book, and to loose the seven seals
thereof" (5:5). When John turned to see the Lion, he saw "a Lamb as
it had been slain." The Lion had prevailed as a sacrificial Lamb. And
the twenty-four elders (representing the complete company of the
redeemed) sang a new song, saying, "Thou art worthy"—and all the
multitude in heaven gave the Lord Jesus a sevenfold ascription of
praise, saying with a loud voice, "Worthy is the Lamb that was slain
to receive power, and riches, and wisdom, and strength, and honour,
and glory, and blessing." And with that praise, "[they] worshiped
Him that liveth for ever and ever."

Jesus, our Lord, with what joy we adore Thee,
Chanting our praise to Thyself on the Throne;
Blest in Thy presence, we worship before Thee,
Own Thou art worthy, and worthy alone.

Lord, Thou art worthy:
Lord, Thou art worthy;
Lord, Thou art worthy; and worthy alone!
Blest in Thy presence, we worship before Thee,
Own Thou art worthy, and worthy alone!

—H. D'A. CHAMPNEY

107

23

That Sweetening Influence

The Lord showed him a tree.
EXODUS 15:25

At this point in history, Israel was a redeemed people. Slavery's chains had been broken, and their foes overwhelmed in the waters of the Red Sea. They were led into a new and living way, which God had opened for them through the place of death. Then they sang praises to God for so great a deliverance. After three days' journey, however, without finding water, they came to Marah, where there was water; but so bitter they could not drink it. There are a few lessons we may learn from this.

THE WORLD HAS A BITTER TASTE TO THE REDEEMED

Right from the beginning of their new life they found the world a wilderness and its waters bitter. Freedom from slavery is surely better than bondage with sweetness, but those who experience salvation can be brought into severe testings which challenge faith. The joy of deliverance soon gave way to murmuring. The many and great benefits bestowed on them suddenly seemed to vanish away, and so did their praises.

Such trials touch vital matters. It would not have been too bad if the problem had been no milk or no wine. Believers can manage without luxuries. But to find no drinkable water was to imperil the preservation of life itself. Marah waters came out of an accursed earth, and this should surely teach us, and be illustrative of the fact, that this earth has nothing at all with which to refresh the souls of a redeemed people. When they most need succor, the world can provide none.

The spirit and temper of the world cannot in any way contribute to Christian life. What springs up from it is gall and wormwood. The motives which govern the world of men no longer appeal to the believer: the lust for money making, the seeking of worldly honor, the attendance at worldly amusements. Nor do true believers find their happiness in worldly company. Among them we have to labor for the bread that perisheth, but their company is not our delight. Most of all, we cannot follow their principles and practices. All these things are now bitter to a man in Christ.

THE FLESH HAS BITTER ENMITY TOWARD GOD

"The people murmured against Moses" (15:24), which was actually murmuring against the Lord. There are times when the Lord's people, having found the emptiness of the world, seek their refreshment from natural causes and fellow mortals. The barrenness of the desert and the bitterness of Marah's waters brought out this deep enmity of the flesh against all that is of God. "Murmur" is an infantile sound, and in days of spiritual childhood it seems natural to murmur against the arrangements and dispensations of God's providence.

In such dire circumstances doubts arise. These were the early days of Israel's deliverance. Instead of a carpet of roses, they found themselves in a wilderness, and instead of the wine of good cheer, they found bitter waters. Perhaps the disappointment is natural since all of the old life is cut off, and murmuring arises from the ground of that disappointment. The new life never becomes a cup of blessing until we have entered more fully into the Lord's inheritance. The trouble with Israel was that they spent forty years in the wilderness when God had made it only an eleven-day experience.

The new life of the redeemed has different tastes and delights and hopes and joys. But it has its trials, simply because it has to exist now in a hostile and not a friendly world. The remains of the flesh in us, not yet crucified, can bring torment and challenge. We may wonder and question why God allows us sickness, sorrow, and bereavement. We perhaps did not expect the failure of our children to walk with us in the heavenward way. The reproach and reviling of those with whom we work can vex the righteous soul! It makes us wonder to see older Christians lose their love for Christ, their conscience blunted in business dealings, their fires of witness burnt out to dry ash, and with no more enjoyment in heavenly things. These are all bitter experiences for newborn souls in Christ.

THE CROSS HAS A SWEET INFLUENCE TO THE SAINT

"The Lord showed him a tree, which when he had cast into the waters, the waters were made sweet" (Ex. 15:25). This was not a tree with which the Bedouins were acquainted, nor would the dwellers in the desert have the slightest idea how to make the bitter waters of the desert sweet with such vegetation. This power is not inherent in any tree. It was something especially imparted by the Spirit of of God to teach a spiritual principle.

The tree symbolizes the cross of our Lord Jesus Christ. The tree was to be cut down, and thus was our blessed Lord on the cross of Calvary.

But the man of God, God's representative, Moses, cast that cut-down tree into the bitter waters. This immediately had a transforming effect: the bitter waters were suddenly made sweet by it.

The Lord Jesus is the Tree of Life in Scripture. It was He who was symbolized by a tree in Eden's garden in the beginning of God's Book. He was figured in the burning bush, which Moses saw in the desert of Midian—the bush that burned, but was not consumed. He was the tree David the psalmist wrote about in Psalm 1: "He shall be like a tree planted by the rivers of water, that bringeth forth His fruit in His season; His leaf also shall not wither" (Ps. 1:3). He is pictured in the Tree of Life found at the end of the Book in the midst of the heavenly Jerusalem, "which bare twelve manner of fruits, and yield-

111

ed her fruit every month: and the leaves of the tree were for the healing of the nations" (Rev. 22:2).

It is this blessed Lord Jesus who is the antidote for all our cares. The tree flung into the bitter waters made them sweet and drinkable and life-giving. Oh, wondrous cross! Glorious cross! Blessed interpreter of the love of God to us. Let it soak into all our trials, vexations, sorrows, bereavements, discontent, and disappointments. It was Marah that taught Israel the sweetness of the tree, and it is only the cross of the Lord Jesus which can sweeten our life here below.

How sweet the name of Jesus sounds
In a believer's ear;
It soothes his sorrows, heals his wounds,
And drives away his fear.

It makes the wounded spirit whole
And calms the troubled breast;
'Tis manna to the hungry soul,
And to the weary rest.

Weak is the effort of our heart,
And cold our warmest thought;
But when we see Thee as Thou art,
We'll praise Thee as we ought.

Till then we would Thy love proclaim
With every fleeting breath;
And triumph in that blessed name
Which quells the power of death.

—JOHN NEWTON

24

The Great God Our Saviour

The great God and our Saviour Jesus Christ.
TITUS 2:13

Together with the Epistle to the Romans, the Epistle to the Hebrews is one of the great doctrinal treatises of the Word of God. The first part speaks of our Lord as being a new and better Deliverer; the second part as having a new and better Sacrifice; the third part as having a new and better principle by which we can be saved—that of faith, not works.

WHO HE IS

The first chapter sets forth our Lord's absolute and certified Deity.

1. He is the "Heir of all things" (1:2). No created being could ever be heir to this vast and illimitable universe.

2. He is the Maker of the worlds (1:2). Worlds here means *ages*. The Son of God framed and designed the different dispensations and brought the whole into existence "by the word of His mouth."

3. He is the Brightness of the Father's glory (1:3). He is the outshining of all that God is. He embodies in Himself every divine attribute and perfection.

4. He is "the Express Image of His Person" (1:3). This means that He is the exact impress of all that God is. As wax returns the exact

impress or image of a seal, so does the Lord Jesus the exact image of all that God is.

5. He upholds all things by the word of His power (1:3). All things move in their own orbits and are held there and move there to exact moments of time—all by the power of the eternal Son of God.

Such is the exalted dignity of the Lord Jesus as the eternal Son of God. This Sonship belongs to essential Deity, not something acquired when He came to earth. He possesses divine attributes, exercises divine prerogatives, and is the emanation of all divine excellence and beauty.

Chapter 2 then shows us His true and proper Manhood:

1. He was made "a little lower than the angels" (2:9). This is a quotation from Psalm 8 in which Messiah's incarnation is prophesied. He was to take upon Him the nature of a creature lower than the angels "for the suffering of death."

2. He was partaker of our flesh and blood (2:14). All that needed to be done for human redemption could only be done by our Lord assuming our nature, or else He could not atone for our sins.

3. "He took on Him the seed of Abraham" (2:16). He must come by way of a particular segment of the human race. It was most fitting to come through Abraham, since the nation issuing from him was to be God's chosen vehicle for His self-revelation and for the accomplishment of His eternal purposes.

4. He "suffered being tempted" (2:18). He was made open to temptation—to feel the force of it—the malignant nature of it—the subtilty of it, though never was He tempted to comply. He could not sin.

WHAT HE DID

1. "By Himself [He] purged our sins" (1:3). Only because He was the infinite God could He absorb the infinite punishment of sin. He did this "by Himself"—no man could lift a hand to help Him do it.

2. He destroyed the devil (2:14). The word "destroy" does not mean to annihilate but to render powerless—to disarm—to make idle. This Goliath of hell fell before the strong Son of God and would

114

never again dare confront Him.

3. He delivered His people from the "fear of death" (2:15). We all fear death. Death is the king of terrors to sinful men, but when we come to Christ, death even becomes a doorman to transport us into the presence of His glory.

WHERE HE IS

He "sat down on the right hand of the Majesty on high" (1:3). This signals a completed work. Here is acceptance by the Father. Here is authority at the Father's right hand where He sat—the place of highest power and authority. Let us look well to Him when we come to worship. Let us see who He is, what He is, and where He is. The Lord Jesus is God within to cheer us—God above to bless us—God who came into our humanity to atone for our sins—God who reigns on high as our Mediator, so that we may present our worship, praise, and adoration to our Father and with His smile of approval.

To the name of our salvation,
Laud and honor let us pay,
Which for many a generation,
Hid in God's foreknowledge lay.
But with holy exultation
We may sing aloud today.

Jesus is the name we treasure,
Name beyond what words can tell;
Name of gladness, name of pleasure,
Ear and heart delighting well;
Name of sweetness, passing measure,
Saving us from sin and hell.

Jesus is the name exalted
Over every other name;
In this name where'er assaulted
We can put our foes to shame:

115

Strength to them who else had halted,
Eyes too blind, and feet too lame.

Therefore we, in love adoring
This most blessed name revere,
Holy Saviour, Thee imploring
So we write it in us here
That, hereafter heavenward soaring,
We may sing with angels there.

—ANONYMOUS (15TH CENTURY)
TR. BY JOHN MASON NEALE

25

A Mighty Contrast

Then did they spit in His face.
MATTHEW 26:67

From whose face the earth and the heaven fled away.
REVELATION 20:11

The spitting took place in the palace of Caiaphas, the high priest of Israel. This was done because of our Lord's testimony that He would come again: "Hereafter shall ye see the Son of man sitting on the right hand of power, and coming in the clouds of heaven" (Mt. 26:64). It was in contempt of this claim that they spat on Him. It was after the high priest had rent his clothes, thinking that he had heard some form of blasphemy rather than the words of Him who was "the Wisdom of God" manifest in the flesh.

More dishonor has been done to the Lord in religious circles than any other place, and the Jews were the most religious of all. God sent forth to men, in incarnate form, His own beloved and eternal Son, and claimed for Him our admiration, love, and reverence. But man spat in His face. Nothing could have done Him greater dishonor.

OUR LORD'S HUMILIATION

"Then did they spit in His face." This is the height of all iniquity.

117

It is the mark of man's greatest shame. And who did this shameful act? The Jews of Jerusalem who were supposed to be looking for Messiah's advent! They were the best educated and, in their own eyes at least, the most devout and religious ones of that elect nation. You might have expected a Turk or a Hottentot to do this, but these were Abraham's seed, who were the best taught of all men in the Book of God, and whose religion was founded on divine revelation. They were not idolatrous Egyptians, or superstitious Romans, or ignorant heathen who had never heard of the living and true God, but men learned in the Scriptures and worshipers of the living God. They represented the natural man at his best with all the influences upon him of knowledge, law, government, and religion.

Spitting on anyone is shameful behavior. But who is this upon whom they spit? None other than the Son of God! Wicked though it would be, one can imagine a man spitting on another who was found out in some heinous crime. I recall a Chinese innkeeper doing this to one of his guests who had been caught in the dead of night stealing from other guests. It would be a still more wicked thing to spit on a holy man, or even a pretended holy man, such as a Hindu sadhu.

But this spitting is upon the Son of God, "the only begotten of the Father, full of grace and truth." It is He who is spoken of in the Scriptures as "the mighty God"—"Immanuel, God with us"— "The Lord our Righteousness"—"God over all, blessed for ever"—"the great God and our Saviour!" Having come into the realm of human life, His goodness shone out like the sun in an unclouded atmosphere. After all the good He did in His earthly life, one would have thought that men would have exclaimed with the Psalmist: "How great is His goodness!" With what gratitude all men should have blessed and praised His name! But alas, they spit in His face.

Why was this? Had He told them He was a mere man like themselves, they would readily enough have believed that. But when He spoke words which told plainly who He was, and when they heard Him ascribe to Himself divine honors and powers, they resented it, and so spat upon Him. Everything He said and did confirmed His Messiahship and confirmed all that Scripture had said about Him.

118

But blindness had happened to Israel and so the representatives of the most religious of all men spat upon Him.

THE LORD'S GLORY

As the Son of God, the Lord Jesus was incapable of elevation. But as the Son of man, He was raised from the lowest humiliation and degradation which sinful men could heap upon Him, to the highest degree of glory. At His resurrection He was declared to be the Son of God with power. At His ascension, the gates of heaven were opened to Him and He was adored, worshiped, and magnified by myriads of angels as He went to sit upon the Father's throne of glory. As the exalted Lord, He is "higher than the kings of the earth," even "King of kings, and Lord of lords" (Ps. 89:27; Rev. 19:16).

In the Revelation, John sees the Lord Jesus in glory. He sees more. He sees what is to come. "From whose face the earth and the heaven fled away." "I saw," said the apostle—and what he saw in the vision is what all unbelieving men are to see in reality by the sight of their eyes. Such men are to stand before that throne of glory, a fearful sight indeed for those who have spit upon Him.

What John saw was a great, white throne. That throne in heaven represented God's supreme rule over all His created works. None can challenge the authority of that throne. None can question the decisions made by the One who sits there. None dare rise against the power of that throne. It is the throne of absolute, universal, sovereign sway.

Its greatness also lies in the fact that all men of every race and age are to be gathered there. It is white because no error can mar it, no injustice can stain it, and no bribe can pollute it. It is a throne of white, unalloyed justice.

John's eyes focused on the Person that sat on that throne. And who did he see there? None other than the same Jesus upon whose face men once spat. The day of His grace, the acceptable year of the Lord, the time of love, is past for unbelievers. This is a throne of judgment for all who have rejected His grace and spurned His love.

But listen to this: "From whose face the earth and the heaven fled

119

away." It is a kind of folding up and putting away of the whole creation: the heavens, because they have been polluted by the sin of angels; the earth, because it has been polluted by the sin of men.

The sight of the Saviour's face in glory is to cause the present earth and heaven to flee away. Think what majesty is in His face to bring about such a phenomenon! Think what power must emanate from Him when all creation, animate and inanimate, cannot abide the sight of His face!

The day of this manifestation in glory is near at hand. He has gone within the veil for a season, but He is to come forth from within the veil. His glorious Person is to be manifested to an extent not known before. That day will find those who have spit upon Him in awesome fright. But to those who have believed and have embraced Him as Lord and Saviour, it will be the wonderful vision which the eyes and hopes and hearts of all true believers long to behold.

> *If here on earth the thoughts of Jesus' love*
> *Lift our poor hearts this weary world above:*
> *If even here the taste of heavenly springs*
> *So cheers the spirit, that the pilgrim sings:*
> *What will the sunshine of His glory prove?*
> *What the unmingled fullness of HIs love?*
> *What hallelujahs will His presence raise?*
> *What but one loud eternal burst of praise!*

—J. G. DECK

26
Three Words Before the Darkness

Father, forgive them; for they know not what they do.
LUKE 23:34

Today shalt thou be with Me in paradise.
LUKE 23:43

Woman, behold thy son!... Behold thy mother!
JOHN 19:26-27

Our Saviour hung on the cross for three hours before the amazing supernatural darkness fell. It was as though He hung suspended there in broad daylight so that all the world might know that He was assuredly nailed there. In that light man made jest of Him. He was "despised and rejected of men," and made the butt of their ridicule. The intensity of man's hatred was there demonstrated. It drew the disguise off man's religious, educated, and civilized face, all of which the Jew represented, and exposed a soul overflowing with all the malignity of wickedness. In these three hours of light, in which the Lord hung a spectacle before all the world, He uttered three of what we call the seven words of the cross.

"FATHER, FORGIVE THEM"

"Father, forgive them; for they know not what they do." This was

121

the divine response to the uttermost of man's wickedness. There was no reproach, no complaint, no condemnation of the crucifiers. The day of God's vengeance was not yet come; this was still "the time of love."

Israel had failed its responsibilities. The nation had proved false to the divine expectation, and purpose. The cross now closed out the former dispensation, and God's dealing with Israel as a special nation was now suspended. But salvation would be open to one and all in that rebellious nation so that a remnant of Israel would be saved.

The Lord judged that "they know not what they do." They were blind to the heinous nature of their offense. Even the earth trembled at their crime, and the heavens frowned with preternatural darkness. The cross reveals man's moral deformity and exhibits his foolishness. It is man's supreme folly, man's greatest offense, and only shows man's utter ignorance of things divine. "Not this man, but Barabbas," they cried. "They hated Me without a cause," said the Saviour. But all man's sin can be forgiven through that very sacrifice the Lord Jesus was making on man's behalf. This is our Lord's prayer—that man may accept the Father's forgiveness. This is what was declared by Peter after the Lord's ascension (Acts 3:17-19).

The cross provided the Lord Jesus with an opportunity more fully to express His love for mankind. Forgiveness is a very big thing and opens the way for every other blessing. When the mountain of sin is removed, then God's favor can be manifested. It takes away the curse of the law and the terrors of future judgment. This forgiveness was so great especially because of the extreme unworthiness of those for whom He prayed. The Jerusalem sinners were the most wicked of all sinners—more wicked even than those of Sodom and Gomorrah.

"TODAY SHALT THOU BE WITH ME IN PARADISE"

"Lord, remember me when Thou comest into Thy kingdom," was the dying prayer of one who first had cast reproaches on the Saviour, while crucified alongside Him. Both thieves had levied their insults. The enmity of wickedness comes out in crucifying our Lord between two wicked men, so as to cover Him with shame and make His name the more infamous. Both were "malefactors"—common thieves. One would expect them to have some feeling of sympathy while suffering the same death. But no! Yet a complete, transforming change came to one of them. In his last few moments, his heart was turned in true repentance and God saved his soul, like one taken as a brand from the everlasting burnings. It was a singular instance of the power and grace of God toward the chief of sinners. It was like David snatching a lamb from the mouth of a lion.

The genuineness of this man's conversion was attested by the fact that first, he judged himself, declaring in a few words his great sorrow for sin—full proof of his sincerity. Secondly, he justified God and rebuked the other reviling malefactor. This was genuine repentance and genuine love, which now shrank from the injustice inflicted on the Saviour. This man knew he deserved to die. As David said, "I acknowledge my transgressions: and my sin is ever before me" (Ps. 51:3).

In justifying God, this thief did so publicly: "We receive the due rewards of our deeds." His confession was in the presence of a multitude of bitterest enemies. He acknowledged his condemnation to be just, and it was made before he made any plea for mercy. That repentance was accompanied by earnest prayer: "Lord, remember me." It was brief enough, but full and comprehensive and issued from his heart.

Then came our Lord's gracious word: "Verily I say unto thee, Today shalt thou be with Me in paradise." It was granted him that day—the same day. He was to be with the Lord among the blessed. In such a marvelous promise he found eternal comfort in the Lord.

"BEHOLD THY MOTHER."

The first woman was deceived in the garden. Here three women, all named Mary, are at the cross, and are there with the utmost sympathy. But these verses have special reference to the Lord's mother, Mary. The Lord at His birth had partaken of her very substance in the flesh. The wise men had given her no worship, and Simeon had blessed only the parents but not the child, for the less is blest of the greater (Heb. 7:7); the less cannot bless the greater, hence Simeon could not bless the child Jesus.

Mary was losing Him, but in the parting He handed her over to the care of His beloved disciple, John. John would provide for her. It was an act of tender love and care.

In one way, the Lord Jesus came into the world as we all come into it—born of a woman. This was a touch of His tender care for womanhood. And "from that hour that disciple took her unto his own home" (Jn. 19:27).

Upon the cross of Jesus
Mine eye at times can see
The very dying form of One
Who suffered there for me;
And from my smitten heart with tears
Two wonders I confess,
The wonder of His glorious love,
And my own worthlessness.

I take the Cross of Jesus
For my abiding place;
I ask no other sunshine than
The sunshine of His face;
Content to let the world go by,
To know no gain nor loss;
My sinful self my only shame,
My glory all the cross.
—ELIZABETH C. CLEPHANE

124

27
One Word Out of the Darkness

My God, My God, why hast Thou forsaken Me?
MATTHEW 27:46

The period of three hours of darkness is the heart of our Lord's redeeming experience. For three hours He had hung on the cross in broad daylight as a spectacle to the world. Then fell a universal darkness when, apparently, the sun was made to withdraw its light by divine order. All the lights of the universe were commanded to go out, as God drew the curtains of mourning for His dear Son.

This darkness was not an eclipse of the sun. No eclipse brings total darkness, nor does any eclipse last for more than a few moments—never three hours. This was something the world had never seen. It drew universal attention to the fact that the Son of God was being crucified. The darkness was both a message of warning and of hope for sinful men. It was God arresting the universe to stand still and ponder this stupendous event happening on earth—the death of the Son of God.

THE MEANING OF THE DARKNESS

Since the world began, no one had ever seen total darkness at any time, much less at noon. It is at noon when the sun is at its meridian, when it shines in all its strength and splendor. This, then, was something extraordinary, far above the course of nature. It would be a most frightening thing for all men everywhere, and would certainly silence the ribaldry of wicked men around the cross who, during the hours of light, had made jest of God's crucified Son.

In the first place, the darkness expressed the wrath of God. Our Lord was made "a curse for us," and was now to encounter the full wrath of God as such. We read that "the wages of sin is death." While the Son of God had no sin of His own and, having none, could not be exposed to death, yet He was standing as our Substitute and, as such, was exposed to that wrath. It was as though the Lord had stepped forward and said, "I take full responsibility for all the sin of mankind and accept the curse laid upon it."

All was now silent. The amazing phenomenon of total and universal darkness frightened to silence the wicked crowd who had made jest of Jesus. In that strange silence and in the blackness of that hour, the Son of God as Son of man was to encounter, without interruption, the awful wrath of a holy God against sin. The cataracts of that divine wrath were now to break upon Him, and the billows of the curse were to sweep over His soul.

From another point of view, this darkness also expressed the powers of hell. "This is your hour, and the power of darkness," said the Saviour some time before (Lk. 22:53). It was an hour given to man to vent all his innate hatred of God and His Son, and for the powers of hell to shroud the world in a thick pall of darkness, as though to hide from man the meaning of the cross, and with it the hope of redemption.

There is still another analogy. This darkness may also be a picture of the love and mercy of God blanketing the world to cover and hide man's shameful sin. The love of God, remember, is not granted in the cross, but commended in it. The cross manifests the love of God, for "while we were yet sinners, Christ died for us"; "[He] loved me, and gave Himself for me." It was, then, as though God cast a thick, black pall over the world so that man should never know the full extent of his wickedness, lest he plunge into the abyss of absolute despair.

126

THE TRANSACTION IN THE DARKNESS

The Lord Jesus was left alone in the darkness. Even His disciples had fled in fear. Toward the end of this period, there came from the Saviour this awful cry: "My God, My God, why hast Thou forsaken Me?" Who can measure the depth of that cry? It is almost sacrilege to attempt it. When we remember that the eternal Son of God was co-equal with the Divine Father and the Divine Spirit, what we witness here is a breach of the eternal fellowship, and this is deeper than human understanding can fathom.

I would dare to believe that, in some mysterious way, the Lord Jesus as the Son of man was still supported by divine strength from the Father and the Holy Spirit. But in respect to any joy or comfort flowing from them, He was left totally bereft. There was a suspension of any communication of comfort or sense of human happiness. The suspension of the whole and entire stock of this divine and heavenly comfort created the sensible lack of it in the soul of the Saviour. Hence the deep thirst for that comfort caused this bitter cry.

We shall never fathom the experience of the Saviour in this darkness. He did not go to hell as to a place, but the wrath He endured was the full sufferings of hell. It is God's wrath that makes hell what it is. The Lord in this period of time consumed, as only the Son of God could, all the sufferings of hell for all men; but at the same time, like the bush which burned before Moses, He was not consumed by the intensity of it.

His union with the Godhead was not actually broken. He did not cease to be the Son of God because He had become the Sin Bearer. The Father still loved the Son; but now, as Judge of sin, He could not spare His Son in the office of a Surety. Jesus was suffering as the accursed of God. But the words, "My God, My God," show us that while the Saviour was denied and forsaken of all sensible comfort from the face of God, yet He endured it all, and faith held fast. The sufferings produced no shadow of doubt in His soul, no unbelief in the righteousness of what He was enduring, and no infirmity which would have made sin possible. God was still His God as the Son of

127

Man, and while His holy soul was brought into the extremity of grief, yet it never reached the point of despair.

By this bearing of divine wrath to the fullest extent, the righteousness of God was vindicated, and out from it came the blessing of our redemption. "I will give thee," says the Lord through Isaiah, "the treasures of darkness" (Isa. 45:3). Oh, what treasures! Oh, what riches! But let us never forget that these treasures were dug out of that deep and awful darkness, and came forth from secret places too fathomless for us to approach. Standing by that very cross, as it were, where the Son of God endured this bewildering and awesome experience, let us bow before Him and give to Him that of which He is so worthy—the tribute of grateful hearts.

> *Behold! Behold the Lamb of God,*
> *On the Cross!*
> *For us He shed His precious blood,*
> *On the Cross!*
> *O hear His all-important cry,*
> *"Eli, lama sabachthani!"*
> *Draw near and see the Saviour die*
> *On the Cross!*
>
> *Behold His arms extended wide,*
> *On the Cross!*
> *Behold His bleeding hands and side,*
> *On the Cross!*
> *The sun withholds its rays of light,*
> *The heav'ns are clothed in shades of night,*
> *While Jesus wins the glorious fight*
> *On the Cross!*

—Joseph Hoskins

128

28
Three Words After the Darkness

I thirst.
JOHN 19:28

It is finished.
JOHN 19:30

Father, into Thy hands I commend My spirit.
LUKE 23:46

We do not find recorded in John's Gospel the three hours of darkness. It was in these three hours that our Lord was forsaken by God. But in John's Gospel the Father is looking on His Son with uninterrupted delight, as bringing to full accomplishment the divine plan for man's redemption. His union with the Father was not dissolved, though all comfort was taken away. The Son of God was beloved by the Father on the one hand, while on the other He was surety and made sin for us. Thus He bore and sustained two relations and two natures in His one person.

In the same way God could act toward Him in two ways in relation to these two. As Christ was our Sin-Bearer, God showed His wrath; as Christ was His eternal Son, the Father showed His love. God sees the latter, even though He hid His love behind the clouds for those three hours. Three words came from the lips of our Lord after the darkness, and they are full of meaning.

"I THIRST"

That was a cry too deep and sore for our feeble understanding. The fact that He was the Son of God did not exempt Him as the Son of Man from pain, nor did it make that pain less real. This thirst was no common thirst. It proclaimed His true humanity, but it was a far deeper thing than the thirst of ordinary mortal men, for behind it was the awful heat of God's wrath, which He had endured through the three hours of darkness. Those who heard this pitiful cry had no understanding of what it meant.

Since every suffering was met with derision, now instead of water "they gave Him vinegar to drink mingled with gall." It was the drink customarily given the crucified to dull the pain. It was a drug.[1] But our Lord "would not drink." He was now past the utter depths of His sufferings, being forsaken of God. This cry was a piercing, agonizing cry from those great depths, just as He was emerging from them. How intense that thirst must have been! Men met it, even after the warning of the darkness, with derision by offering drugged vinegar—what mockery!

But within this cry was the heart's desire for renewed fellowship with the Father. The rich man in hell had cried for water. He, too, thirsted. But he was in hell forever because he could not swallow down the wrath due to sin except by enduring it forever. That is why a sinful man cannot be released from hell. He can receive the wrath of God, as it were, only in small portions, all of which are intolerable enough. But our Lord swallowed down in a few hours all the hell due to man's sin—all that man cannot consume even throughout eternity. His soul was so large as to have the capacity for all of that wrath. Who, then, could measure the heat of those three hours on the cross in the darkness? It was the bearing of this which produced this cry, "I thirst!"

1. This drink was given, not out of some act of kindness to the crucified, but to keep the sufferer from going into shock, and therefore dying sooner.

130

"It is Finished"

This is but one word in the Greek, "Finished." It was the second word spoken by our Lord after the darkness. Having swallowed down the full measure of the wrath of God, He had, in fact, suffered the substance of the second death—the ultimate of death. In a sense, therefore, redemption's price was now paid, and was actually so when the heavens were closed to him. God's face was turned away from Him, and the cataracts of divine justice poured over Him as man's Sin-Bearer.

We see in Adam that sin had several effects. The moment he sinned he died spiritually, immediately. That very moment he was separated from God. But His body died progressively. That body did have to die. So in the cross of our Lord there were these two aspects in the consequence of bearing sin. He suffered the spiritual separation first, when He was cut off from sensible communion with the Father. But there would have to be that physical death, too, when He would enter the realm of death to conquer it for us.

What was finished? He had endured the full wrath of God for human sin. It was that which was now finished. That which could not be swallowed by man, though he drink from the cup of it forever, was endured by our Lord in those three hours of darkness. Now it was finished. No more wrath was left in the cup. He had drunk it to the dregs.

Having done this, and having finished the last drop of the wrath of God, there must of necessity be a renewal of that fellowship and communion with the Father, which had been suspended for us.

"Father, into Thy Hands I Commend My Spirit"

Our Lord was now brought into the greatest degree of comfort and composure of spirit by renewed communion with the Father. This was now His support with which to enter the last act of the drama. The sunshine of His Father's face had broken through again, so that He could look up and say, "Father."

His last loud cry, therefore, was no longer one of anguish, but

131

relief. No man had taken His life away. True, man crucified Him, but could do no more without His consent. He now laid down His life in the final act of sacrifice that He might take it up again in sovereignty. "I have power to lay it down, and I have power to take it again" (Jn. 10:18).

I recall reading what a prelate wrote in an issue of *Time* magazine: after thirty years or more of study, he had concluded that the Lord died of asphyxiation. He must have researched among human causes only—certainly not in the Word of God, which alone can interpret the things of God. In asphyxiation there is a struggle for breath. In crucifixion there can be, admittedly, this kind of death. But the head would be thrown back in its fight for breath. Now, when our Lord had finished the whole of what He was called upon to endure, He gently, quietly laid His head on His own breast and dismissed His spirit. This was a most unique act which only He could do. Having completed the sacrifice, by His own choice He stepped out of this life into the realm of death to destroy the last enemy, death itself.

> *When I survey the wondrous Cross*
> *On which the Lord of Glory died,*
> *My richest gain I count but loss,*
> *And pour contempt on all my pride.*
>
> *See from His head, His hands, His feet,*
> *Sorrow and love flow mingled down;*
> *Did e'er such love and sorrow meet,*
> *Or thorns compose so rich a crown?*
>
> —ISAAC WATTS

29
The Greatness of Christ

He is Lord of all.
ACTS 10:36

The most immense thing that ever took place in the universe is that the Son of God brought deity to humanity. The immensity of a believer's life is that we are brought into living union with One who is so great—so pure—and so holy. And by His exaltation, the Lord Jesus has taken humanity with Him back to the throne of God. There He sits, awaiting the day when we will join Him there. The immensity of this union is realized all the more when we contemplate the greatness of the One to whom we are united.

HIS GREATNESS AS THE SON OF GOD

"Who is the image of the invisible God" (Col. 1:15). Being the express image of Godhood, He could therefore say, "He that hath seen Me hath seen the Father" (Jn. 14:9). The greatness of His Person makes for a humbling attitude in our souls. Thus Abraham considered His greatness and the sight of it reduced him, as it were, to dust and ashes: "Behold now, I have taken upon me to speak unto the Lord, which am but dust and ashes" (Gen. 18:27). When we remember who He is—the Creator of the worlds—the Lord of all—we are astonished that He should set His love upon such vile creatures.

His Greatness As Heir of All Things

God has spoken to us by His Son "whom He hath appointed heir of all things" (Heb. 1:2). He was that before the worlds were made. All things were made "for Him" to exhibit His glory. Now they are redeemed for that same purpose so that "He might fill all things." All things are to revert to His control. Thus those who are joined to Him are made "heirs; heirs of God, and joint-heirs with Christ" (Rom. 8:17). "Hearken, my beloved brethren, hath not God chosen the poor of this world rich in faith, and heirs of the kingdom which He hath promised to them that love Him?" (Jas. 2:5). O blessed state!

His Greatness As the Hope of the Ages

"For the creature was made subject to vanity, not willingly, but by reason of Him who hath subjected the same in hope, because the creature itself also shall be delivered from the bondage of corruption into the glorious liberty of the children of God" (Rom. 8:20-21). Men cry out in hope. They are "prisoners of hope" (Zech. 9:12). The whole universe cries out in hope. There is an enigma—a puzzle—a quandary—a contradiction—something wrong with the whole universe, and it cries out in hope. Nothing is left hopeless. But that hope is only in the Lord. "Thou art my hope, O Lord" (Ps. 71:5). In Christ alone is hope—hope for the nations—hope for Israel—hope for the Gentiles—hope for the whole universe.

His Greatness in the Eyes of the Father

"Thou lovedst Me before the foundation of the world" (Jn. 17:24). "Therefore doth My Father love Me, because I lay down My life, that I might take it again" (Jn. 10:17). "This is My beloved Son, in whom I am well pleased" (Mt. 3:17). The Old Testament is full of figures of that love which the Father has for the Son, such as in Adam when God walked and talked with him in Eden—in Abraham and his love for Isaac—in Jacob's special love for Joseph—all of which are faint reflections of God's love for His beloved Son.

HIS GREATNESS IN HIS OWN NATURE

"Holy, harmless, undefiled, separate from sinners, and made higher than the heavens" (Heb. 7:26). "Holy"—having absolute purity; "harmless"—having no ill-feeling toward any; "undefiled"—having no stain of dishonor on His obedience, or imperfection in His love toward God and man; "separate from sinners"—not of the same sinful stock. That He was all this was acknowledged even by demons who called Him "the holy One of God" (Mk. 1:24). He was never touched by the curse of sin. Heaven knows it. Earth knows it. Hell knows it. No one ever pointed to a flaw in His character.

HIS GREATNESS IN THE WORK OF REDEMPTION

"Who His own self bare our sins in His own body on the tree" (1 Pet. 2:24). And how many sins has even one person? Since each sin has its own measure of punishment, who can measure the degree of punishment for all the sins for all people? It is said that He should "taste death for every man" (Heb. 2:9), which means our Lord died millions of deaths in His one death. Since hell was the punishment deserved, then He suffered millions of hells in that one cry—"The pains of hell gat hold upon Me" (Ps. 116:3). Through His substitutionary sacrifice on the cross, He has obtained for His people "the remission of sins." Through that finished work of redemption, He has made it possible for God to give eternal life to as many as should believe on His name.

HIS GREATNESS IN THE BESTOWMENT OF GRACE

Personal unworthiness is no obstacle to His "so great salvation." None can find Him unwilling or unable to save. "Ho, everyone that thirsteth, come ye to the waters…without money and without price" (Isa. 55:1). "Jesus stood and cried, saying, If any man thirst, let him come unto Me, and drink" (Jn. 7:37). No unworthiness can bar the way to Him. His mercy and grace are incomparably great and sweet. This will be the eternal song of the redeemed.

135

O Lord, enlarge our scanty thought
To know the wonders Thou hast wrought;
Unloose our stammering tongues to tell
Thy love immense, unsearchable.

How can it be, Thou heavenly King,
That Thou shouldst us to glory bring;
Make slaves the partners of Thy throne,
Decked with a never-fading crown?

Our hearts then melt, our eyes o'erflow,
Our words are lost; nor will we know,
Nor will we think of all beside,
My Lord, my Love is crucified.

Firstborn of many brethren Thou;
To Thee, lo! all our souls we bow;
To Thee our hands and hearts we give:
Thine may we die, Thine may we live.

—NICOLAUS VON ZINZENDORF
TR. BY JOHN WESLEY

30
Joy in Worship

Enter into His gates with thanksgiving, and into His courts with
praise: be thankful unto Him, and bless His name.
PSALM 100:4

I will joy in the God of my salvation.
HABAKKUK 3:18

Those of us who have traveled in foreign lands have been shocked
at the lewd, licentious abominations men worship. In God's calling
Israel to be a vessel for His own revealings, we see how different was
their worship to that of the nations around.

Israel was called to worship the living God "in the beauty of holiness." Each mercy from God brought forth louder praise. Gratitude
expanded their adoration. As God's goodness fell in increasing show-
ers, so the heat of devotion ascended in higher flame. David, in the
psalms of worship, rises to great heights of exuberant joy before the
Lord. He soars high on the wings of adoring praise to God's holy
name.

It was never intended that worship be morose, and the skies over
the head of a worshiping people be full of somber gloom. David even
danced with joy before the Lord (2 Sam. 6:14), overcome with
delight in his God. Worship was robust, not anemic; virile, not life-

137

less; spontaneous, not forced. There was a natural overflowing of the heart in worship. "O come, let us sing unto the Lord: let us make a joyful noise to the rock of our salvation" (Ps. 95:1).

JOY IN GOING UP TO GOD'S HOUSE

It ought always to be a joy to anticipate worship, to go where the Lord is in the midst. It is surely the full grant of blessedness to meet the Lord, the living God, and our Saviour. In Old Testament times this was expressed in Israel as going up to mount Zion (see Jer. 31:6).

It was so different from Sinai. It was at Sinai they heard the law. It spelled out God's will, what must be if they would be accepted by Him. "This do!" and life is purchased—heaven is won. If man shares God's holiness, then he may ascend God's throne. But man failed, and hope from self died forever. The broken law frowns terribly upon men. It claims its payment. It utters its inexorable curse. Perfect obedience is its due. One breach makes it a foe forever.

But Zion's mount is in the Promised Land, and symbolizes God's system of grace. It is bathed in perpetual sunshine. It calls men to come and meet with God. All your males shall appear before Me in Zion, and three times a year they came! "The joy of the whole earth, is mount Zion" (Ps. 48:2). Zion means "Projection." It was in the world, but rose out of the world, jutting into the heavenlies. It represented a heavenly position, a heavenly consciousness, a heavenly hope, a heavenly education, and a heavenly joy.

As they climbed Zion's mountain, the Israelites sang Psalms 120 through 134. These are called "psalms of degrees" or "of ascent." On the earthly level, Israel was a divided and scattered people, but Zion drew them together. The higher they climbed, the nearer they came to one another, until, on the top, they were together and sang: "Behold, how good and how pleasant it is for brethren to dwell together in unity!" (Ps. 133:1). Unity is not a mere organizational thing. It is the outcome of spiritual ascent into our heavenly things in Christ. And the higher these people climbed Mount Zion with God's house in view, the louder sounded their praises. This response to God, and their ascent of Zion, was a most joyful experience. "O send out Thy light and Thy truth: let them lead me; let them bring me unto Thy holy hill, and to Thy tabernacles. Then will I go unto the altar of God, unto God my exceeding joy" (Ps. 43:3-4). If Israel had such joy in going up to Zion's hill to the house of the Lord, surely we believers of this dispensation have greater reason for joy in going to meet our God.

JOY IN GOD'S HOLY PRESENCE

The last psalm in that special group of psalms is 134, and this they sang when on top of the mount in His holy presence. "Behold, bless ye the Lord, all ye servants of the Lord." No longer were their hearts cold, dead, rank with nature's weeds. They were now warm; faith sprang to life in them. They were in the house of God to adore and praise the beauties of the Lord. It was a grand reality of joy and bliss. What a lively, happy feeling it is to be where God's presence is manifested and realized.

We read that in those days: "It came even to pass, as the trumpeters and singers were as one, to make one sound to be heard in praising and thanking the Lord; and when they lifted up their voice with the trumpets and cymbals and instruments of music, and praised the Lord, saying, For He is good; for His mercy endureth for ever: that then the house was filled with a cloud, even the house of the Lord...for the glory of the Lord had filled the house of God" (2 Chron. 5:13-14). Exultant souls brought down the glory of the Lord.

We live in an era when God is known and worshiped as the Father of all who believe. Believers in the finished work of Christ Jesus are in a closer, more intimate, and more settled relationship with Him on the ground of redemption than Old Testament saints. The Holy Spirit has been given, the fruit of His life is joy, and His enabling help is the power for worship. What a joyous experience it should be, then, to be within the veil, in the presence of God, accepted by Him, made complete in Christ! Where are words to testify the joy of faith? The Spirit pauses and exclaims: "Unspeakable" (1 Pet. 1:8).

The Lord Himself is the believer's overflowing cup. We have access to His smile. The weary rest on His loving breast. The full

139

heart can know no greater joy, than pure, grateful worship of the Father and the Son.

> *O for a thousand tongues to sing*
> *My great Redeemer's praise,*
> *The glories of my God and King,*
> *The triumphs of His grace.*
>
> *Jesus! the name that charms our fears,*
> *That bids our sorrows cease;*
> *'Tis music in the sinner's ears,*
> *'Tis life, and health, and peace.*
>
> *Hear Him, ye deaf; His praise, ye dumb,*
> *Your loosened tongues employ;*
> *Ye blind, behold your Saviour come;*
> *And leap, ye lame, for joy.*
>
> —CHARLES WESLEY

31
The Proclamation in the Supper

Ye do show [proclaim] the Lord's death.
1 CORINTHIANS 11:26

The Lord's Supper is central to the Christian faith. It is very close to the spiritual affections of believers, and greatly treasured by those who know its value. It is one of the two ordinances which the Lord intended for the Church during His absence.

The first is baptism, which is an individual responsibility, and a once-for-all act. The New Testament never contemplates an unbaptized believer (or a baptized unbeliever). It is good to be a believer, but it is better to be a baptized believer.

The second ordinance is the Lord's Supper, and this is a corporate act, which should be observed with constant regularity. The remembrance feast must not be relegated to a secondary or inconspicuous place in the life of the assembly, much less set aside completely.

In this feast, believers look backward to the cross and remember the Lord's sufferings in their place. They look upward to heaven and remember that the Lord is risen, and that He is meat and drink for the sustenance of their present life in Him. They look forward and remember that He is coming again to receive them to Himself.

The observance of this feast is something which the Lord has requested us to keep: "This do!" Rarely did the Lord ask His people to do anything by way of commandment, but this He did, for very important purposes. His wisdom is clearly seen in such an assignment. We should, of course, obey without the injunction, and without perceiving such wisdom. Ours is not to question the Lord's commands, but to trust and obey.

But then, the Lord does not treat us as slaves, to be commanded without understanding. Rather does He treat us as friends with whom He shares His sovereign counsels, and to whom He explains His ways so that believers may more whole-heartedly cooperate with Him in carrying out His instructions.

THE HISTORICAL INSTITUTION

This institution is given us in Matthew 26, Mark 14, and Luke 22. The prime emphasis is to remember Him in His death. Had it been left to His people to choose a memorial, some might have chosen a mighty miracle, a favorite parable, a song, a notable discourse. But no! The emphasis is placed by our Lord on His death, on the offering up of Himself on our behalf. The Lord thus imprinted His sacrificial death as central to the whole system of divine truth. This was the wisdom of God, for we, alas, are prone to forget that very thing.

In the course of Church history there have been dark ages, days of spiritual declension, when our Lord's death was not the Church's main emphasis. That sometimes shifted to a lust for temporal power, by means of which the Church could raise up or depose kings of the realm; or to social reform; or to the making of creeds and credentials.

These things are never central. That which is central is that which is unique—the substitutional and sacrificial death of the Lord Jesus. Happy the fellowship of believers who maintain that emphasis! The Lord did not come to earth primarily to relieve poverty by providing a bread ticket. Nor did He come primarily to instruct our ignorance. He came to deal with the fact and issues of sin, and make possible through His sacrifice the removal of our sins, reconciliation to God, restoration to His favor.

The course of Church history has produced ministers, so-called, who deny the deity of Christ, His Godhood, His atoning death, and

His bodily resurrection. They suggest that these ideas were invented by the Apostle Paul, that the Lord never claimed to be God, that His death was merely a noble example of self-sacrifice, that His body of flesh and bones never did come out of the tomb.

The institution of this feast confounds all these unholy breathings. It gives the lie to all such suppositions. His deity is evident in what He Himself said at the feast—in what His death would accomplish. Not even Moses, in his greatest flights of illumination, ever dared suppose that his death could remit sin. "This is My blood," said our Lord, "which is shed for many for the remission of sins" (Mt. 26:28). No other blood but His blood could avail to take away sins.

THE DIVINE INSISTENCE

Matthew seems to go out of his way to show that this memorial feast did not originate with the Church, or with any apostle. He tells us that when the feast of the Passover was near, Jewry's rulers said, when plotting His death, "Not on the feast day, lest there be an uproar among the people" (Mt. 26:5). But our Lord said, in effect, "on the feast day" (v. 2), so that the type of the slain paschal lamb should have its fulfillment in Him on that God-appointed day. These things of God are never in the hands of men.

Then, again, the wisdom of our Lord in placing the emphasis on His death is seen in what took place in the house of Simon the leper (Mt. 26:6-13). Simon's house would be shunned by the supposedly clean, but the undefilable Lord went to eat with Simon. For Him no infection could touch, and all diseases must obey. While in Simon's house, "There came unto Him a woman having an alabaster box of very precious ointment, and poured it on His head, as He sat at meat."

When one complained: "To what purpose is this waste?" the Lord defended the woman, saying, "She did it for My burial." She knew what the disciples were so slow to believe: that He must die. To emphasize again the primary importance of remembering His death, He shifts the emphasis from the poor "for ye have the poor always with you; but Me ye have not always." Poverty is no barrier to being saved, or to entering Heaven—but sin is. Therefore, far more impor-

143

tant than social reform and the relief of poverty is our Lord's death on the cross, without which no man can be saved and enter heaven.

"Verily I say unto you," said the Lord Jesus, "Wheresoever this gospel shall be preached in the whole world, there shall also this, that this woman hath done, be told for a memorial of her." Here was a woman with the right emphasis, as in the words of dying Jacob in Genesis 49:18, "I have waited for Thy salvation, O Lord." O wondrous, glorious cross! O wondrous death of Thine, Lord Jesus! Help us ever to remember it, and hold it in the primary place.

> *I am not worthy: cold and bare*
> *The lodging of my soul;*
> *How canst Thou deign to enter there?*
> *Lord, speak, and make me whole.*

> *I am not worthy; yet, my God,*
> *How can I say Thee nay,*
> *Thou, who didst give Thy flesh and blood*
> *My ransom-price to pay?*

> *O come, in this sweet hallowed hour,*
> *Feed me with food divine;*
> *And fill with all Thy love and power*
> *This worthless heart of mine.*
> —H. W. BAKER

32

Love, Righteousness, Wisdom, Power

Whom God hath set forth...to declare His righteousness.
ROMANS 3:25

Hereby perceive we the love of God,
because He laid down His life for us.
1 JOHN 3:16

O the depth of the riches...of the wisdom...of God.
ROMANS 11:33

Christ the power of God.
1 CORINTHIANS 1:24

In the days when our Lord was here on earth, the cross was a Roman means of death. But the cross was abhorrent to the Roman. The victim was associated with evil, and represented a degraded and disgraceful specimen of humanity. The cross was looked upon as associated with ignominy, crime, and weakness.

But the cross of the Lord Jesus changed that! His cross was neither an accident nor a mere expression of the malice of men. It was a God-planned cross, His plan for human redemption. Since it is by works we express what we are, then, since the cross is God's greatest work, it must be the greatest revelation of His character.

The apostles gloried in our Lord's cross. Since it wrought redemption for fallen man, it became the symbol of life, hope, and blessing. It is at His cross that fallen man hears the joyful news of salvation, a gospel unheard of in hell, but which has fallen on our ears—the sweetest melody we have ever heard. It is written by God's own pen in the Scriptures of truth—fixed, eternal, and divine. Every attribute of God has concurred in erecting it. There is no defect in this divine plan, no blemish, no decay.

THE CROSS: THE LOVE OF GOD

"In this was manifested the love of God toward us, because that God sent His only begotten Son into the world, that we might live through Him. Herein is love, not that we loved God, but that He loved us, and sent His Son to be the propitiation for our sins" (1 Jn. 4:9-10). The salvation of man has come out of God's great heart of His unmeasured and immeasurable love.

Every stone in this edifice has been shaped by love and laid by love. The supreme expression of that infinite love is that His beloved Son came down from heaven, was born in Bethlehem, lived in Nazareth, died at Calvary, descended into the grave, burst the bands of death, rose into heaven, and now sits at the right hand of God. He did all that because He loved us!

There are certain experiences in human existence which have the tendency to challenge the love of God. We witness the violence in nature: the calamity of earthquakes, floods, droughts, hurricanes, pestilence—and such things afford opportunity for the evil in the heart of man to challenge God's love. Or we go through the trials of social and family life, disfiguring and crippling infirmities, prevailing and ravaging sicknesses, the incidence of poverty and misery, and finally, death. And we wonder: Does God really love us? Why has God allowed this to come to us? These things blow up the smoke of unbelief. They tend to bring to man the bitterness of despair and a sense of hopelessness in the battle of life.

But whatever challenges these things may bring, we look at the cross and know, beyond a shadow of doubt, that God loves us. In giving His Son to die for us, God gave everything He could give. "Hereby perceive we the love of God, because He laid down His life for us" (1 Jn. 3:16). Here is love immeasurable in its breadth, and length, and depth, and height: "the love of Christ, which passeth knowledge" (Eph. 3:19). "God is love."

THE CROSS: THE RIGHTEOUSNESS OF GOD

"Christ Jesus: whom God hath set forth to be a propitiation...to declare His righteousness" (Rom. 3:24-25). God is a God of law. The natural world is founded on the Creator's governing laws. God has written moral law on the tables of the human heart. If God would save man, then salvation must answer to His own holy law. Forgiveness must be based on righteousness. However much God may love, He cannot wink at sin or fail to punish it.

When God's holy law examines His beloved Son in His personal life, it can find no fault in Him. He comes forth in all the glory of pure sinlessness. No cleansing is needed for Him. Hence "the righteousness of Christ"—His own personal righteousness—is what He Himself is. Perfection finds embodiment in Him. His every aspect is righteousness, without a single flaw. He has no stain. Sin could not touch Him. Earth witnessed Him as the sinless Son of man.

But when He stood forth to answer for *our* sins, to take full responsibility for them, and bear the punishment for them, then the law saw Him as a sin-laden Person, and Justice cried: "Awake, O sword, against My shepherd, and against the Man that is My fellow [equal], saith the Lord of hosts" (Zech. 13:7). The law must now condemn Him. The law must afflict Him and put Him to grief. The law must erect a cross and hang Him on it—to be "made a curse for us" (Gal. 3:13). The law must require His precious blood. Why? Because God is righteous, and any forgiveness must be based on righteousness, or else it would never answer to the justice of God. It would never bring peace to the conscience. It would never silence the accusations of Satan.

In Old Testament days, as we see in Romans 3:25, God could only cover sins in the symbolic sacrifices of Judaism, "For it is not possi-

147

ble that the blood of bulls and of goats should take away sins" (Heb. 10:4). But our Lord was "the Lamb of God, which taketh away the sin of the world" (Jn. 1:29)—even those sins which had been only covered in times past.

Where are our sins now? They have been taken away where they cannot be found. They are out of reach (Ps. 103:12); out of sight (Isa. 38:17); and out of mind (Heb. 8:12). Thus believers cannot be condemned. Faith in the Lord Jesus casts away all misery with one hand, and with the other grasps eternal joy and happiness.

THE CROSS: THE WISDOM OF GOD

"The preaching of the cross is to them that perish foolishness" (1 Cor. 1:18). That wondrous cross has no charm for an unbeliever. It is a sad, sad thing that unbelief has so blinded the eyes of men that they see no beauty in the Lord Jesus, and no value in His sacrifice. The altogether lovely One is not lovely to them. He who is the essence of preciousness is vile to their sin-clouded eyes. God's grandest gift is scorned by them. Heaven's glory is cast away like "a root out of a dry ground" and as a husk to the wind.

But in the cross of Christ our Lord we see the fruit of God's omniscient mind. It is the expression of the eternal thought of God which is absolute wisdom. When Paul was at Corinth, he saw that the cross was foolishness to the intellectual Greek. Pride in such men must find a way to God more suitable to the supposed dignity of man. They turn from the revealed plan and wisdom of God to grope in the darkness of their own conceits. They place their puny reason above the counsels of the Most High God, who alone is all-wise.

What a delusion sin has brought to man! The intellectuals of this world don't know that all they have is unenlightened reason. No light from heaven shines into man's darkened mind. Sin has dragged reason through the dust so that man cannot know the things of God. The natural man can only mind earthly things.

Out of this unenlightened reason, pride rises up to make man walk in a vain show. He feels neither sin nor the need of pardon. Like Cain, he dares to come before God with the fruit of his own toil, and proud-

148

ly trample on the blood offering of the Saviour. The blood of Christ is offensive to his taste. He thinks he has need of nothing. Thus pride closes his eyes; he cannot see the Lord. It closes his heart; he will not receive Him.

How, then, do we see the wisdom of God in the cross? It lies in the perfect concurrence of His love and justice. On the one hand, God loved man and desired to save him. On the other hand, His justice required that each sin of man be punished. How could God save man? What means could produce such a saving work?

It is here that God's wisdom is displayed in devising a means whereby "He might be just, and the justifier of him which believeth in Jesus" (Rom. 3:26). His devised means is in the cross! Till this is seen, the soul of man will never see God's salvation, never see how sins are washed away, never see how the gates of hell are shut, how the door of heaven is opened, never enjoy the eternal rest of God.

The Cross: the Power of God

"Unto them which are called, both Jews and Greeks, Christ the power of God" (1 Cor. 1:24). "Unto us which are saved it is the power of God" (1 Cor. 1:18). The cross is not just an objective display of God's love, righteousness, and wisdom. It is designed for a very practical purpose—that of saving men. It is God's means by which He can bring many sons to glory and make them eternally joyful, eternally happy, eternally peaceful.

Thus God the Father gave His beloved Son and sent Him to be the Saviour of the world; and God's beloved Son completed the work of redemption by drinking up the cup of wrath which man's sin deserved. But He has also sent forth the Holy Spirit to knock on the barred doors of man's heart. For this purpose the Holy Spirit assails the fortress of self-love, reveals the perils of sin, and points the penitent to the cross of Jesus our Lord so that he may shelter in the sure refuge of the cross.

The cross is raised on earth to save men. It takes the power of God to do that! There is no sin of man so crimson but that it cannot be washed away by the precious blood of Jesus. There is no sinner so far

149

away from God that he cannot be found and brought home again. That is the power of God! There is no remaining sin so deeply entrenched in a believer's heart that it cannot be overcome and stripped of its power.

Through the cross God gives forgiveness to the guilty, peace to the conscience-stricken, cleansing for the defiled, victory for the defeated, relief for the burdened, rest for the weary, courage to the faint, confidence to the dying, and comfort to the bereaved. The cross of Christ has all that power, and much more. It is "the power of God."

> *Jesus, Thy blood and righteousness*
> *My beauty are, my glorious dress;*
> *'Midst flaming worlds, in these arrayed,*
> *With joy shall I lift up my head.*
>
> *Bold shall I stand in that great day,*
> *For who aught to my charge shall lay?*
> *Fully absolved through these I am,*
> *From sin and fear, from guilt and shame.*
>
> *Lord, I believe Thy precious blood,*
> *Which, at the mercy seat of God,*
> *Forever doth for sinners plead,*
> *For me, e'en for my soul, was shed.*

—NICOLAUS L. VON ZINZENDORF
TR. BY JOHN WESLEY

33
Immeasurable Sufferings

My God, My God, why hast Thou forsaken Me?
PSALM 22:1

Behold, and see if there be any sorrow, like unto My sorrow.
LAMENTATIONS 1:12

There is nothing in the whole of human literature more poignant
than Psalm 22. It is the ultimate depth of suffering, a prophetic portrayal of the pouring out of our Lord's soul unto death. This psalm
was committed to "the chief singer," as the title indicates, for none
but he could have charge of such a holy strain. The *Aijeleth Shahar*
in the title is interpreted as "the hind of the morning"—a figure of
Christ, the promised Messiah. It is another portrayal of our Lord
under the figure of this gentle animal being pursued and hunted by
ferocious beasts.

It is a psalm of the cross, and expresses in detail, as nowhere else,
the sufferings of our Lord on that shameful tree. There is no psalm
like this psalm. One of its most remarkable features is the absence of
any confession of sin. The sufferer has no personal sin to be confessed, and this because it points to the sinless Son of Man.

There are a number of beasts mentioned:

There are "bulls" in verse 12. The bull was a ceremonially clean
animal, and no doubt this points to the Jewish rulers, scribes, and

Pharisees, high priests such as Annas and Caiaphas, and the whole Jewish Sanhedrin which plotted to put Jesus to death.

Verse 20 speaks of "the dog." The dog was an unclean animal and this refers to the Gentiles, often spoken of as "Gentile dogs" by the Jews. Rome was in charge of Palestine at the time of our Lord's death, and He was condemned by the Roman governor, Pilate, to die a Roman death. Roman soldiers, too, circled the cross and gambled for His garments.

Verse 21 speaks of "the lion's mouth," also an unclean animal, and probably points to all the hosts of hell as ferocious and fearful enemies, aligned with the prince of demons, who "as a roaring lion," seeks those whom he may devour. They were to fling themselves upon the Lord in His moment of greatest physical weakness in the hope of tearing Him to pieces.

Then, in verse 21, "unicorns" are mentioned, and scholars have interpreted this as single-horned rhinoceros. It may well be a representation of death itself and its enormous power to impale men.

THE UTTER DERELICTION OF OUR LORD

The first source of our Lord's sufferings was in relation to God: "My God, My God, why hast Thou forsaken Me?" (v. 1) or, "Why hast Thou let Me go?" or "Why hast Thou given Me over?" It is the cry of One who had been in eternal communion with God, but now finds that communion is being sundered. It is not a rebellious cry. It is not a cry of complaint. It is one of bewilderment. Why? The answer is really given in verse 3: "But Thou art holy." At this point of time, our Lord was being "made…sin for us," taking responsibility for all our sins which were laid upon Him. Thus the Father, in His office as God, had to turn away from the sight of His Son, who was now in His role of Sin-Bearer on our behalf.

The second source of our Lord's sufferings was in relation to man. The ribald mockery of men is depicted in verses 7 and 8: "All they that see Me laugh Me to scorn: they shoot out the lip, they shake the head, saying, He trusted on the Lord that He would deliver Him." Priest and people, Jews and Gentiles, soldiers and civilians are all seen in this derisive laughter, which summed up a universal scorn for God's beloved One. And together with this mocking ribaldry were gestures of contempt, such as the shooting out of the lip, wagging the head, and other obscene gestures. Then came what may have been the cruelest part—the taunting of His faith in God, which must have been like poisoned venom to His holy soul.

The third source of our Lord's sufferings was in relation to the powers of hell. Satan marshaled all his forces and cleverly waited to attack until our Lord was brought into the most bitter extremity of physical pain: "All My bones are out of joint." It is said, I believe, that there are about two-hundred bones in the body, and who can measure this kind of suffering when all were dislocated? It was at this strategic hour that Satan flung all his forces against Christ, hoping to overwhelm Him.

The Glorious Jubilation of Our Lord

From that deep and dire dereliction, the psalm passes into the triumph of the Saviour, and thus into a paean of praise. I will mention three wonderful results because the Lord Jesus bore our sufferings:

(1) The creation of a gospel for sinful men—a gospel of redeeming love. "I will declare Thy name unto My brethren" (v. 22), that is, the name of God, who is just. Through the sufferings of the cross, the just God found the righteous means of becoming "the justifier of him which believeth in Jesus" (Rom. 3:26). Here, too, the Church of firstborn ones comes into view, when the Redeemer says, "In the midst of the congregation will I praise Thee" (Ps. 22:22). He leads the praise of His redeemed ones before God the Father.

(2) The provisions of a complete satisfaction for such believing people. "The meek shall eat and be satisfied: they shall praise the Lord that seek Him: your heart shall live forever" (v. 26). They who believe are meek in that they have renounced all human pride, and have sought after the Saviour until they found Him.

(3) The fruition of our Lord's passion gathered from all nations. "All the ends of the world shall remember and turn unto the Lord: and all the kindreds of the nations shall worship before Thee" (v. 27).

They shall remember, return, and revere the Lord.

The last phrase of the psalm is for the glory of God: "He hath done this" (v. 31), which, I understand, is but one word in Hebrew— "finished." This has reference, not only to the completed work on the cross, but to the completed work in believers as they are finally presented to Himself "not having spot, or wrinkle, or any such thing."

> *Mercy and truth unite,*
> *O 'tis a wondrous sight,*
> *All sights above!*
> *Jesus the curse sustains!*
> *Guilt's bitter cup He drains!*
> *Nothing for us remains,*
> *Nothing but love.*

> *Love that no tongue can teach,*
> *Love that no thought can reach:*
> *No love like His.*
> *God is its blessed source,*
> *Death ne'er can stop its course,*
> *Nothing can stay its force;*
> *Matchless it is.*

—THOMAS KELLY

34

The Altar's Sweet Savor

Noah builded an altar unto the Lord...
And the Lord smelled a sweet savor.
GENESIS 8:20-21

The sanctifying power of God's grace is demonstrated for us in the lives of godly believers of the past. The new world upon which Noah stood after the flood was, in a sense, resurrection ground. On this ground Noah, the man of God, now builds. As with every true child of God, his life has a new beginning in redemption and is characterized by joy in praise and prayer through reconciling blood.

THE ALTAR'S SWEET SAVOR

Noah and his family had built an ark which was scorned by the world. But he built it in obedience to God and entered it with calm confidence to find peace and safety within. Now that the flood had abated, God spoke again, "Go forth of the ark," and Noah left it on Ararat with the old world a veritable graveyard, but a new world visible before his eyes. The riot of evil was past; the new is at rest.

NOAH'S FIRST EMPLOYMENT

"Noah builded an altar unto the Lord." Worship was his first employment. The last trace of judgment had passed away. The new earth was to be filled with what came out of the ark. But coming forth into this new world, there was much work to be done. There would need to be a house for his family and stalls for his cattle. The necessities of existence demanded that he begin immediately to plan and build. But Noah gave God the first place in his new life. The first building was an altar; his first act, the exercise of worship.

Thus we are taught the primacy of worship. Those who are truly redeemed are first drawn to this sacred exercise. It is the first concern and comes before all that is to contribute to earthly existence. Thus we see for the first time an altar raised. The ground before the flood was cursed, but judgment made it clean.

THE ALTAR OF SACRIFICE

The altar itself was a figure of Christ in His Godhood. Only He, because He was God, could bear the weight of human sin. The purpose of the altar was to hold up a sacrifice to God. No multitude of angels could have borne such a weight. Only Deity was sufficient, and it was Deity alone in the Lord Jesus which held the sacrifice intact on Calvary's cross when He was forsaken. He was strong in His own divine right, immovable in His own Godhood.

If the altar set forth our Lord's deity, then the sacrifice on it was symbolic of His humanity. "Who His own self bare our sins in His own body on the tree" (1 Pet. 2:24). Who could count the number of sins? The sins of the whole human race must have been as many as the sands of the seashore. Who but God could absorb all the punishment due them?

Thus our Lord, as the true Altar and Sacrifice, could answer for all our sins. Let no man vainly imagine that we weak mortals can contribute in any way, or carry any of this burden. "Christ is become of no effect unto you, whosoever of you are justified by the law; ye are fallen from grace" (Gal. 5:4). It is not Christ with angels, or the Church, or penance, or purgatory, but Christ and Christ alone.

THE SWEET SAVOR OF THE OFFERING

"The Lord smelled a sweet savor." Noah's sacrificial offering

156

pointed to Calvary's cross. It is His sacrifice alone which rises to God as a sweet savor. His sacrifice satisfies every attribute of the divine nature.

It is a sweet savor to God's *justice*. Justice calls for obedience without faltering and without interruption. Where there is disobedience, then justice demands death. It cannot connive at evil. But in our Lord's sacrifice there is that which meets every demand of justice so that it is honored with full satisfaction.

It is a sweet savor to God's *truth*. Truth can never wink at evil or pretend it is not there. Nor can it restrain from exposing and denouncing it. Neither tears, nor prayers, nor penances can deflect truth or cause truth to become untruth by excusing sin. But in the sacrifice of God's beloved Son, truth smells a sweet savor and is fully satisfied.

It is a sweet savor to God's *holiness*. Holiness cannot look on iniquity or any form of uncleanness. It is of purer eyes than to behold what is impure. But at the cross, where the precious blood of Christ flows and cleanses from all sin, even holiness joys in that sacrifice and smells a sweet savor.

This sacrifice of our Lord's is the joy of heaven. It delights every attribute in the Godhead. Then let it be *our* joy. Let it refresh our souls as we celebrate it.

> *Lowly Jesus, mighty God,*
> *Suffering Lamb and stricken Dove,*
> *In the wrathful winepress trod,*
> *Who can tell Thy wondrous love?*

> *Sin-abhorring, holy Word,*
> *Cursed for sin, how didst Thou prove*
> *Fiery pangs of judgment's sword!*
> *Bruised—profound, amazing love!*

> *Floods of love like rivers, spilled*
> *From the Bosom judgment clove,*

157

All God's universe have filled—
Fragrant, deep, atoning love!

From Thy wondrous Cross alone
Bruised Lamb and wounded Dove,
All God's radiancy hath shone:
Thou art all our Light and Love!

—FRANK ALLABEN

35
Jesus in the Midst

They crucified Him, and two other with Him, on either side one,
and Jesus in the midst.

JOHN 19:18

There are several occasions when our Lord is spoken of as being
in the midst. At the age of twelve, He was found in the temple "sitting in the midst of the doctors" (Lk. 2:46). According to His own
promise, He is "in the midst" of those who gather in His name (Mt.
18:20). After His resurrection, He came and "stood in the midst" of
His disciples (Lk. 24:36). In John 19:18, He is on the cross between
two thieves. In a future day, He is seen as a Lamb "in the midst" of
heavenly glory (Rev. 7:17). The discerning spiritual eye can readily
envisage many scenes where this is true. Some of these truths make
the gospel a seed of life, a garden of pure comfort, a textbook of
redeeming love.

IN THE MIDST OF ANGELS AND PROPHETS

Concerning our Lord's life of redeeming love here on earth, we
read: "Which things the angels desire to look into" (1 Pet. 1:12).
Angels have lofty intellects, but the cross of the Lord Jesus baffles
their understanding. It is beyond them. They peer, probe, search diligently, and are utterly amazed at seeing the sovereign Lord of glory

159

in the poor garb of our human nature, at witnessing His stooping into the mystery of death—His dying so cruel a death for such undeserving rebels as we are. It simply astounds them.

Then, again, here on earth in Old Testament times there were prophets inquiring into the same mystery: "Of which salvation the prophets have inquired and searched diligently, who prophesied of the grace that should come unto you" (1 Pet. 1:10). God told out His plan in figures, types, and illustrations. Strong efforts were made by God to break down ignorance, to introduce pure light, to open up His way of salvation. So types and figures were profusely given. Every kind of figure was used to picture the coming Christ. The Spirit of God caused the prophets to speak thus of the Redeemer for whom they searched most diligently. Thus our Lord was central in the midst of all inquiries, both of angels above and prophets below.

IN THE MIDST OF GOD AND SINNERS

When we contemplate God in His majesty, we see on His head the crown of pure and holy excellence. He is a just God. He has on record all our sins. God would cease to be a just God if there were in Him any compromise with evil. Justice in His nature demands that we pay what we owe.

The sinner has nothing with which to pay. We have nothing of our own but sin. Our attempt at payment would never lessen the vast amount of debt we owe for all our sins, no more than the removal of a daily grain would wear out the ocean sands.

The Lord Jesus comes in the midst of God and sinners, and in one sum discharges the whole debt. The claim against us ceases; the prisoner goes free. Justice revels in the cross, and God and man are reconciled through His blood. The Saviour puts His hand on both God and man, and the gulf which separated them is spanned by Him.

IN THE MIDST OF THE OLD AND NEW COVENANTS

The old covenant was a covenant of works. Man did not place that covenant in his heart but under his feet. He touched it only to break it and scatter it to the winds. The privileges under that covenant were instantly forfeited. We are not to dream idle dreams, as some do, that this covenant of works still stands, and that man can live through it and be justified by it. That is a foundation of sand.

The new covenant is a roll of divine blessings. It is clearly set forth in Jeremiah 31:33-34. It includes for the believer: sanctification of spirit, adoption into God's family, divine light, and eternal pardon. The believer may claim all these as God's covenant pledge. But how can God, who is so high and holy, whose very being is perfection, whose home is eternity, contract with man who is so low, so vile, so loathsome—the offspring of all corruption?

The answer is that the Lord Jesus is in the midst. The covenant rests on His work. It is written in unfading letters of eternal love, and is based upon God's unchangeable purpose in His Son. It is made with Jesus as our Representative. He stands in the midst.

IN THE MIDST OF FRIENDS AND FOES

Friends were few at the cross. John, Mary Magdalene, the mother of Jesus, and another, were about all that were left—a few who loved Him.

But His foes were many. The priests were full of hate; they still were stung by the Lord's rebuke about their making clean the outside of the platter. They gnashed their teeth at His inveighing against their useless ceremonials which were mere play-acting.

Pilate was wilting under fear of his master, Caesar, afraid of losing his job and the political goodwill of the Jews. Herod the king was mocking—a carnal, adulterous "fox," as the Lord called him. The crowd was superficial. Those who had cried "hosanna" were now crying "crucify" as though He were the basest of men. The soldiers—hardened gamblers—were at the foot of the cross, throwing dice for His vestments. But Jesus is in the midst, and because He is, some, like the centurion, will cross from the company of His foes to the circle of His friends.

IN THE MIDST OF SAVED AND DAMNED

When Joseph was in prison, two notable offenders were by his

161

side. Human judgment discerned no difference. They were objects of the Pharaoh's displeasure, and both expected an ignominious end. But one mounts the path of favor and is crowned with honors; the other is left in bonds to perish (Gen. 40).

This is a signal to the distant wonders of the cross. There is a corresponding circumstance. Two thieves are crucified, one on either side of our Lord. But as they writhe in torment, Jesus is in the midst. A change takes place in one as great as light from darkness, life from death. He loathes the sin which he had fondled. He confesses its malignity. He looks to Jesus and cries: "Lord, remember me," that is, "Lord, I am perishing. Only Thou canst save me!" And saved he is! "Today shalt thou be with Me in paradise." The other perishes—hardened by his sufferings. Hell was near, but he neither saw, nor feared, nor shunned it. It has well been said, "A man may be lost, though close to Christ when he meets death; a man may be saved though close to death when he meets Christ."

> *Jesus! That name is Love,*
> *Jesus, our Lord!*
> *Jesus, all names above,*
> *Jesus, the Lord!*
> *Thou, Lord, our all must be;*
> *Nothing that's good have we,*
> *Nothing apart from Thee,*
> *Jesus, our Lord!*
>
> *Righteous alone in Thee,*
> *Jesus, the Lord!*
> *Thou wilt a refuge be,*
> *Jesus, our Lord!*
> *Whom then have we to fear,*
> *What trouble, grief, or care,*
> *Since Thou art ever near?*
> *Jesus, our Lord!* —JAMES G. DECK

36
The Accomplished Mystery

My meat is to do the will of Him that sent Me,
and to finish His work.
JOHN 4:34

It is finished.
JOHN 19:30

The Bible is God's spiritual paradise. In this garden of God believers love to sit down in those choice spots which are thickset with the redolent blossoms that are fragrant with the Saviour's love; where they drink from everlasting springs; where they feed on the regaling fruit of everlasting redemption.

The mystery of the Saviour's cross is too profound for us fully to understand. But there is a wonderful perfection and glory in it which satisfies every desire of the heart and mind of God. It is a finished work—not merely done, but perfectly done—absolutely and totally accomplished. In His final moments on the cross, the Lord Jesus was fully conscious that His cross work had been perfect in its operation, and that its purpose had been fully achieved.

THE FACT ACCOMPLISHED

The Lord Jesus had been sent by the Father to do a particular

163

work. That work was not to deal with the circumference of things—the ills of society—but to deal with the central cause of all those ills, which is sin. Nothing could remove sin but His death on the cross. From His wounded side and pierced hands, from the cross on which He died, that altar on which He made atonement, there was to flow blood which was to do just that!

That blood was so mighty in its efficacy, so cleansing in its power, that it would wash away every stain of iniquity. His great sacrifice thus became a fathomless ocean of merit which all men everywhere could freely use, and in which all their sins would disappear forever.

This is what the Lord Jesus accomplished on Calvary's cross. He dealt with the fact and issues of sin, broke the chains which bound men, and delivered us from that final end of sin which is hell.

No believer can now be given over to Satan. He owes no debt since the Lord has discharged it all. He cannot receive the wages of wrath because they have been paid by his great Surety in his place. He cannot be kept out of heaven because the Lord Himself has clothed him with the robe of divine righteousness. He may advance to the very throne of God, and there he will find God's acceptance of him. He is free to be one of the citizenry of heaven. All this is an accomplished fact.

The Office Fulfilled

The Lord Jesus was God's sent Messiah—the Christ, the Son of the living God. Three titles were bound up in this title of Messiah, and all were fulfilled in God's Son.

He is the Prophet: the One who is the eternal Word of God, and who, therefore, speaks to us with absolute authority, "Verily, verily, I say unto you!" When He speaks, it is with finality. Nothing can be added. Nothing He ever said has had to be corrected or improved. The Lord never used such words as "perhaps" or "maybe." Whether He was speaking of God, man, redemption, death, eternity, what is after death, or whatever—His were the words of absolute knowledge, the words of divine omniscience.

He is the Priest: "the one mediator between God and men" (1 Tim.

164

2:5). Sin had alienated men and destroyed fellowship with God. To become the true Priest, the Lord must offer this sacrifice for sin and remove it by full atonement. What a mighty load! Could He sustain them? The claims of justice formed a long roll. Could Jesus pay all? Indeed He could! For in Him "dwelleth all the fullness of the Godhead bodily" (Col. 2:9). Sin called for expiation. No sinner could approach a sin-hating God without a sin-removing sacrifice. Jesus became such a Priest with such an offering.

He is the King: Though men mocked His kingship, and objected to Pilate's "accusation" over His head, He is King nonetheless. And not only King but King eternal, King of righteousness, King of peace, King of kings and Lord of lords. Men crowned Him that day with thorns; God has crowned Him with glory and honor.

THE BLESSING BESTOWED

The cross has a threefold blessing. First, it *delivers from sin*. Sin was man's ruin. It drove man from happy fellowship with his Maker. It changed a loving child into a hardened rebel. It made the heart of man a nest of unclean birds, a spring of impure streams, a whirlpool of tumultuous passions, a hotbed of ungodly lusts. But the cross has overcome sin and made possible "the forgiveness of sins" (Eph. 1:7). Sin has no more dominion over those who are saved by the Lord; they are no more its slaves.

Secondly, the cross *delivers from shame*. Sin not only bowed man down, but it filled him with shame. As soon as Adam sinned, he hid from the presence of the Lord. He was ashamed to meet God, ashamed to stand in the light of His holiness. But the cross of Christ lifts up our head so that we may say, "In the Lord have I righteousness." Such a believer can knock at heaven's door without a blush, and with an irrefutable plea.

Thirdly, the cross *delivers from sorrow*. Sin brought many cares to man, and made woman to lie down in many sorrows. The fact of trials—afflictions, sickness, pain, suffering, and death—has driven many into deep depression and despair. But through the cross, such things have been transformed into purifying and sanctifying agents;

165

tools to sharpen and polish believers as stones for the New Jerusalem. Through the cross, sorrow can now become blessed sorrow, and in it we have the soft and tender comfort of our Lord's consoling grace.

Awake, my soul, to joyful lays,
And sing thy great Redeemer's praise:
He justly claims a song from me,
His lovingkindness, oh, how free!

He saw me ruined by the Fall,
Yet loved me, notwithstanding all;
He saved me from my lost estate,
His lovingkindness, oh, how great!

When trouble, like a gloomy cloud,
Has gathered thick and thundered loud,
He near my soul has always stood,
His lovingkindness, oh, how good!

—SAMUEL MEDLEY

37
The Search for Worship

The Father seeketh such to worship Him.

JOHN 4:23

THE FATHER

It is God the Father of whom the Lord speaks to the Samaritan woman—the One who is God in nature and Father in relationship. The name Father seldom occurs in the Old Testament and never there in the New Testament sense. As used in the Old Testament, the word The Triune God is spoken of as a "Father," Jehovah's relationship to the nation of Israel as their Head (see Deut. 32:6; Isa. 63:16; Jer. 31:9). In our Lord's words to the Samaritan woman, He is speaking of God as the Fountainhead of all created things in heaven and in earth—the Father of all spirits, the Source of all humanity, the God of the spirits of all men, the great God our Creator.

When our Lord says that "God is a Spirit," He does not mean some cold, distant abstraction—a mere assemblage of divine attributes—but a God of life and love with the heart of a father and with all a father's resources and rights. True, men have broken that relationship and strayed like a prodigal into a far country, but that does not change God's nature, though it does alter man's relation to Him and the treatment man receives from His hands. He put the

167

fatherly heart in all men and did so after the likeness of His own. It is that fatherly heart which yearns over wayward creatures.

THE FATHER SEEKS

The word "seeketh" means more than appears. God the Father is in search of something which to Him is very precious and valuable, something which He cannot bear to lose. Great as God is, there are some things He cannot think of letting go. It is the very greatness of God which manifests itself in His loyalty to His creatures and His longing for a loving relationship with the ones He has created.

So when anything of man is lost to Him, He searches for it. He would not part with it. God is no cruel tyrant who says: "I have lost a certain thing in man, but I can do without it." Others may overlook something they lose, but not God. "Can a woman forget her sucking child?...Yea, they may forget, yet will I not forget thee" (Isa. 49:15). God cannot forget man. He seeks the lost.

We must not dilute this expression and say God will have us back if we will come, that He will accept our worship if we care to give it. That is far short of the meaning of Scripture. We might ask, But what can God want? Yet we read that He seeks, He seeks something here on earth and from His creatures. What He seeks is the worship which has been lost to Him and which has impoverished man who no longer worships God.

THE FATHER SEEKS WORSHIPERS

God is in search of many things lost to Him by man's default: affection, allegiance, reverence, and obedience, but primarily worship. This is what He especially claims. From man, whom God has created, there should arise without ceasing the fragrance of holy worship. As the Lord even answered Satan: "Thou shalt worship the Lord thy God, and Him only shalt thou serve."

It grieves God that man through sin has been ruined so that he cannot engage in this best of all exercises. But He seeks to have it restored. Does it seem a small thing to you that God should lose the worship of men when He has the worship of myriads of angels? Then

168

you are wrong! God misses every person alienated from Him. This concerns God; it should concern us. Everything we do concerns God, but most of all He is concerned about our worship. And is not His desire enough to provoke us to come to Him with our adoration, since He has made a way back to Himself through the cross of His dear Son? His search is worldwide; His call is universal.

The shepherd misses a lost sheep more than the sheep misses the shepherd. The shepherd does the seeking, not the sheep. The woman loses her coin. It does not miss her, but she cannot afford to be without it, so she seeks it. The father loses a son. He is troubled. The prodigal may not miss his father, but it is the father who runs to meet his son on the road home.

God is in earnest. The One who seeks worshipers is worthy to be worshiped. He desires worship from men here on earth, as well as from angels in heaven. But the worship He seeks is spiritual worship. The outward man is nothing. He wants the inner man of the heart— the innermost shrine. Worship must arise from the depths of a man's soul, but it can rise only through redemption. Forms, robes, gestures, and ornaments are not worship, nor do they help worship. If anything, they hinder it. God wants our hearts.

It is the blood of Christ which can purge sin from us, remove the guilt, and free our soul from dreading God, so that man, through such grace, can give to God true worship. The blood of Christ satisfies God's righteousness and the sinner's conscience. The Spirit of God renews the penitent man in truth. In this way we may give to God what He is seeking—the true worship due to His holy Name.

Praise ye the Father! Praise our God most holy,
Who cheers the contrite, girds with strength the weak!
Praise Him who doth with glory crown the lowly,
And with salvation beautify the meek!

Praise the Father! Source of all our blessing,
Before whose gifts earth's tidiest boons wax dim!
Resting in Him, His peace and joy possessing,
All things are ours, for we have all in Him!

169

Praise ye the Father! Praise ye Him who gave us,
In full and perfect love, His only Son!
Praise ye the Christ, who died Himself to save us!
Praise Father, Son, and Spirit! Three in One!

—LADY MARGARET COCKBURN-CAMPBELL

38
Participation in the Lord's Supper

Take, eat...Drink ye all of it.
MATTHEW 26:26-27

We read of the institution of the Lord's feast in the Gospels, the celebration of it in the Acts of the Apostles, and the exposition of it in the Epistle to the Corinthians. In the institution of it, we read how the Lord first took bread, blessed it, and broke it (Mt. 26:26).

THE FIRST MENTION

One of the most important principles of interpretation is the law of first mention. The first mention of bread and wine in Scripture is in Genesis 14:18, "Melchizedek king of Salem brought forth bread and wine: and he was the priest of the most high God." Melchizedek is one of the most outstanding types of the Lord Jesus, and here he meets Abraham with bread and wine. Abraham had been in battle, and was worn and weary with the struggle. But through Melchizedek he was refreshed with bread and wine.

In this we see a picture of our Lord's tender compassion for His people's needs. With royal bounty, He presents every supply which our wasted strength, sinking spirit, and failing heart require. The fight of faith is fierce; the journey of life often seems long. But at every step a banquet house is open, and food and drink are spread

171

before us. Thus here in His feast there is the spiritual food of His own body given, His own blood shed. Our true Melchizedek invites us to draw near.

If we exclude this incident and look for the mention of the first making of bread, we would find that in Genesis 18:3-6, where Abraham, visited by the Lord in human form and with two attendants, thus addresses the central figure of the three: "My Lord…pass not away from thy servant…And I will fetch a morsel of bread…And Abraham hastened into the tent unto Sarah, and said, Make ready quickly three measures of fine meal, knead it, and make cakes upon the hearth."

The fine meal is the same as that spoken of in the meal offering of Leviticus 2. This fine meal speaks of our Lord's impeccable character. There are no lumps, there is no unevenness, in that holy character. He comes forth in all the beauty of sinless manhood.

But fine meal, too, is only formed by the crushing of the grain when the grinding mill reduces it to powder. The meal then is kneaded, and this speaks of the persecutions of men, their abuse of our Lord's holy body. He is the bruised God-man, broken to make us whole. The kneaded bread was then baked "upon the hearth" of fire, showing us in picture how through suffering our Lord became "the living bread" for our souls.

THE BELIEVER'S PARTICIPATION

In the institution of this feast, our Lord did four simple things with the bread. He took it, blessed it, broke it, and then gave it to His disciples. In doing so He said, "Take, eat; this is My body. And He took the cup, and gave thanks, and gave it to them, saying, Drink ye all of [from] it."

The point to note is the believer's participation in this. He was to partake both of the bread and of the wine, consuming the elements. There is something more in this than simple reflection and remembrance of the historical event of the Lord's death. The feast was the token of the new testament. The beneficiaries of a testament only receive the inheritance after the testator's death. All the benefits of the Saviour's promises thus are now available to believers because Christ has died.

There is a beautiful picture given us in Luke of the believer's participation in the feast. The disciples said, when considering the passover, "Where wilt Thou that we prepare?" And the He said to them, "Behold, when ye are entered into the city, there shall a man meet you, bearing a pitcher of water; follow him into the house where he entereth in. And ye shall say unto the goodman of the house, The Master saith unto thee, Where is the guest chamber, where I shall eat the passover with My disciples?" (Lk. 22:9-11)

Jerusalem was a hostile city, already crimson with the blood of the prophets. The heart of the rulers was filled with hatred. They could not pity; they would not spare. "Come," said they, "let us kill him" (Mt. 21:38). Jesus' emblems had no charm for them. The altogether lovely One was never lovely in their eyes. The all-precious was counted vile. God's grandest gift was scorned.

But here, amidst the world's hostility, was one man who would prepare a place for the Lord in his home. The place was the best he had—a large upper room furnished and prepared (Mk. 14:15). So it came to be that in this man's home the Lord, after beginning the Passover feast, moved it into His own remembrance feast as a memorial of His approaching death, the fulfillment in Himself of the slain paschal lamb of Jewish history.

Thus are we to partake. The best place in our heart's affections must be reserved for Him. We must come with hearts made ready. Let us remember that we live in a hostile world, a world full of enmity and hatred toward God's beloved Son. In the world lies sin's intense malignity. It is a cage of every foul bird, the nesting place for every impurity. We must loathe that world which slew our Lord and pierced His heart. Away with that which spared not Christ our Lord!

Nothing will help believers keep pure and wholesome more than the constant partaking of this remembrance feast. It warms the frigid atmosphere of this world. It will help you climb adversity's hill. It will enable you to struggle with resisting tides. It will revive and invigorate you each time you partake with a true heart. In these days, when the faith of many is found in soft attire, and there is much loitering in slothful ease, oh, let us be like this man in Jerusalem, ready with the best he has for the entertainment of the Lord—a joyful participant in this spread feast of love!

> *O blessed, living Lord,*
> *Engage our hearts with Thee,*
> *And strike within the answering chord*
> *To love so rich and free!*

> *To know Thy loving heart!*
> *To cleave to Thy blest side!*
> *To gaze upon Thee where Thou art,*
> *And in Thy love abide!*

> *Be this our one desire,*
> *Thyself our object here,*
> *The goal to which our hearts aspire—*
> *To meet Thee in the air.*

—JAMES BOYD

39

Three Aspects of the Cross

*Suffer it to be so now: for thus it
becometh us to fulfil all righteousness.*
MATTHEW 3:15

*Put on the new man, which is renewed in knowledge after the image
of Him that created him.*
COLOSSIANS 3:10

*For this purpose the Son of God was manifested, that He might
destroy the works of the devil.*
1 JOHN 3:8

The cross was not an end in itself. It was God's means of producing the Church. The Church was to come forth from the sufferings and death of our Lord, as the woman, Eve, Adam's bride, came forth from his opened side during a deep sleep.

THE GODWARD ASPECT OF THE CROSS

We often forget, or do not realize, that the first work of the cross was to secure the rights of God in righteousness. No divine purpose could come into being without having a basis in righteousness. God's eternal thought was the Church, but the Church could not be built on any ground but that of righteousness. Thus before our Lord began His ministry. He came first to be baptized by John in the river Jordan.

John would have refused Him, but the Lord said, "Suffer it to be so now: for thus it becometh us to fulfil all righteousness."

This had to be settled first, and the essence of righteousness is a total abandonment and obedience to the will of God. An illustration of this is seen in Abraham's offering of Isaac. It was the noblest act of Abraham's life. "Take now thy son...and offer him for a burnt offering (Gen. 22:2). No furnace was ever so hot. But Abraham neither questioned, argued, nor held back. He rose early to obey. Therefore, said God, "Because thou...hast not withheld thy son, thine only son: that in blessing I will bless thee, and in multiplying I will multiply thee" (Gen. 22:16-17).

When our Lord came into this world, He did so, saying, "I come to do Thy will, O God" (Heb. 10:9) "I delight to do Thy will" (Ps. 40:8): "Not My will, but Thine, be done" (Lk. 22:42). That was absolute abandonment to the will of God. But in God's mind that was the cross. Why? Because only through the cross could all unrighteousness be removed and the ground cleared for God to erect a new building, a holy temple of regenerate souls. Thus, through the cross, God obtained His rights in righteousness, which could only be obtained by the utter removal of all unrighteousness. That would include the high treason of God-abandonment, which is the ultimate fruit of unrighteousness. Hence the cry: "My God, My God, why hast Thou forsaken Me?" (Mt. 27:46) That swept the ground clean and gave God a site, so to speak, upon which He could build His Church.

THE MANWARD ASPECT OF THE CROSS

The Lord also could only build His Church with righteous material. The Church could never be composed of man as he is by nature. Man is utterly unrighteous. We have only to look within to find that sad plague. We are lost property to God. Sin has stripped us naked of all righteousness. "There is none righteous, no, not one" (Rom. 3:10). That "old man" as he is called, can have no place in the Church of God's building.

But God has sent forth His Son, that through His sufferings and death at the cross there may be a removal of all unrighteousness from man. Man must stand at that cross in total self-abandonment and abhor himself as a lost, ruined, and guilty sinner. He has no power to help himself. By faith he looks up to Christ as Saviour. There He sees healing for his soul in Him. "In the Lord have I righteousness," he says, believingly. Then he comes to God with an unanswerable plea: "In Christ, my Saviour, my law-abiding Surety, I bring the righteousness of God." And God accepts him. He has put on Christ; he is seen as righteous in Christ. He is material for the building of God's Church.

THE SATANWARD ASPECT OF THE CROSS

"For this purpose the Son of God was manifested, that He might destroy the works of the devil." There is such a being. He is not an empty name, but a mighty power. "The prince of this world," he has enslaved mankind and his sway is global. All are His bondslaves and none can escape by themselves. He is the god of this world, and sets up every system of idolatry to draw worship away from God.

The cross brought utter defeat to this evil one. Seeing our Lord in physical weakness on the cross, he flung all the forces of hell at Him, hoping to overwhelm Him. But the Lord "having spoiled principalities and powers...made a show of them openly, triumphing over them in it [the cross]" (Col. 2:15).

The cross destroys the work of Satan. It removes all the ground of Satan's further work. He can do nothing on God's ground. The cross deprives him of that. Thus the Church is built on safe ground, against which the gates of hell cannot prevail.

> *The Church's one Foundation*
> *Is Jesus Christ her Lord:*
> *She is His new creation*
> *By water and the Word;*
> *From heaven He came and sought her*
> *To be His holy bride;*
> *With His own blood He bought her,*
> *And for her life He died.*

177

Elect from every nation
Yet one o'er all the earth,
Her charter of salvation
One Lord, one faith, one birth:
One holy Name she blesses,
Partakes one holy food,
And to one hope she presses,
With every grace endued.

'Mid toil and tribulation,
And tumult of her war,
She waits the consummation
Of peace for evermore;
Till, with the vision glorious,
Her longing eyes are blest,
And the great Church victorious
Shall be the Church at rest.

—SAMUEL J. STONE

40
Accursed of God

He that is hanged is accursed of God.
DEUTERONOMY 21:23

There is no more terrifying word in human language than that of being made a curse, and especially cursed by God. Surely this must be the extremity of all possible misery, pain, anguish, and despair. One can bear much distress if it is accompanied by the blessing of God. There are many of God's dear people who quietly, patiently, and even joyously bear the burden of intense suffering. But what if there is no blessing? What if, instead, it is all a terrible display of God's wrath? Who can weigh what awful anguish and misery must be wrapped up in the curse of God?

THE CURSE

Sinners are under the curse of God's righteous law. We must fully understand what this curse means. It springs from disobedience. There was no such thing as a curse until sin came in. This earth should never have known the curse. Man had the choice to obey, and power from God to help his obedience. But with the disobedience of the first man, the father of all the human race, his entire progeny passed into the realm of the curse.

This is something which lies on every soul. It is very humbling to

179

be told we are rebels in God's universe, that we are a fallen, corrupt, and polluted people. But we are weighed in God's balances of absolute holiness, and are found wanting. "Cursed is every one that continueth not in all things which are written in the book of the law to do them" (Gal. 3:10). This is as plain as can be told. It brings under its curse every rank and condition of man. The poor cannot be exempted. The learned cannot devise an excuse. All who have been born of Adam's sinful stock have fallen short of God's standard and broken His laws. Thus all are exposed to the curse of the law.

THE SUBSTITUTION

"He that is hanged is accursed of God" (Deut. 21:23). This word does not apply to every man who has been hanged. Even some innocent people have been hanged. In times of persecution many have been crucified by wicked conquerors. It was a Roman means of death to those who resisted surrender. This word has particular application to God's beloved Son, who came to bear God's curse on our behalf. Moses showed prophetically that God's sent Redeemer would hang upon a tree. His sufferings and death on the cross would absorb all the punishment which the law demanded for all our sins.

This was the plan of our loving God from eternity. This is the outflow of God's grace—God's way to save men, and the only way He could save them on the basis of righteousness. But this is an awful sentence when applied to God's beloved Son: "He that is hanged is accursed of God." It tells in the simplest prophetic terms that God's beloved Son would appear on earth and expire on the tree. That is God's pledge, and so it must come to pass in the fullness of time.

It is history now. We of this late generation look back and gaze on the fact of it—that the Son of God was lifted up, a spectacle to God and men, an outcast from heaven and earth. Had Israel been masters of their own house in our Lord's time, they would have wanted to subject Him to a Jewish death by stoning. But God's decree brought about Jewish subjection to the Roman Empire, and crucifixion was their cruel invention. Thus the prophecy, made nearly two thousand years before our Lord appeared, was fulfilled in Him. Jesus hangs,

180

accursed of God—made a curse for us. The whole curse of God upon mankind's dreadful sin, and in all its totality, fell on the sinless Son of God.

THE ISSUE

"Christ hath redeemed us from the curse of the law" (Gal. 3:13). That, then, was the price of human redemption. He bore our sins, and this was the divine decree from before the foundation of the world. This is the deep meaning of the cross and the essence of God's covenant of peace with rebel sinners. There was no coercion on the Son of God to do this. He did it because His infinite love was set upon the sons of men. All our iniquities were laid on Him. All our breaches of God's holy law were charged to His account.

Thus all believers are released from any charge the law can make, or any accusation Satan may rehearse before God. Every transgression of thought, word, and deed has been fully answered and atoned for. All has been suffered by our Lord in order that we should never suffer. These are the eternal counsels of God's infinite mind.

We can never suffer what our Surety has already borne for us. We cannot be placed in double jeopardy. The law cannot exact its punishment a second time, or else it would become unrighteous in itself. Thus we are safe and secure forever because of what our blessed Lord and Saviour has suffered for us. Think what would have happened to us if He had not done that! Ours would have been the curse forever. Then let us rise and bless the Lord, swelling the praise that will continue forever.

O Sacred Head once wounded,
With grief and shame weighed down,
Now scornfully surrounded,
With thorns Thine only crown,
How art Thou pale with anguish,
With sore abuse and scorn!
How does that visage languish
Which once was bright as morn!

What Thou, my Lord, hast suffered
Was all for sinners' gain:
Mine, mine, was the transgression,
But Thine the deadly pain.
Lo, here I fall, my Saviour!
'Tis I deserve Thy place;
Look on me with Thy favor,
Vouchsafe to me Thy grace.

What language shall l borrow
To thank Thee, dearest Friend,
For this Thy dying sorrow,
Thy pity without end?
O make me Thine forever!
And should I fainting be,
Lord, let me never, never
Outlive my love to Thee.

—BERNARD OF CLAIRVAUX

41
Three-Fold Preciousness

*The trial of your faith, being much more precious
than of gold that perisheth.*
1 PETER 1:7

Ye were...redeemed...with the precious blood of Christ.
1 PETER 1:18-19

He is precious.
1 PETER 2:7

Persecution broke out after the martyrdom of Stephen. The world was mad in its hate as it has ever been. Believers were trodden as the mire beneath ungodly feet, and those who escaped death were scattered abroad. In his epistles, Peter writes to those of the *diaspora,* and one of the words he uses over and over again is the word "precious."

PRECIOUS FAITH

In 1 Peter 1:7, he mentions the trial of faith as being precious, and in 2 Peter 1:1, he says that faith itself is precious. Man's frown and persecution's threat give deadly wounds. We read in Bible history of many a tyrant's wrath, of the burning fiery furnace, of the den of raging lions, of stonings and imprisonments. The way to heaven is often in the face of murderous artillery.

183

But faith can overcome! Multitudes upon multitudes with robes of white and palms of victory and songs of endless praise follow the Lamb wherever He goes. They do not fear what man can do to them. Faith untried, unproven, is faith uncertain. The quality of the metal is ascertained by what it can do and bear. The courage of the soldier is evidenced only in the field of battle. The depth of the root of a tree is shown only by its resistance to a storm. Rock is solid only if it stands against all the surges of a raging sea. A foundation is strong only when it remains unshaken in crisis.

Trials do more than test the strength of faith. They consolidate and invigorate it. Its sinews become more firm. Those to whom faith has been given are not to count it strange that they have to swim against the tide. The trial is precious. It makes faith exceedingly precious. We are "to count it all joy when [we] fall into divers temptations."

PRECIOUS BLOOD

"Ye were not redeemed with corruptible things, as silver and gold…But with the precious blood of Christ" (1 Pet. 1:18-19). His blood was not the polluted blood of a man of Adam's race. Our Lord did not come into the world by man, but the body prepared for Him was conceived by the Holy Ghost.

Blood is the symbol of life. "The life of the flesh is in the blood" (Lev. 17:11). The life of the eternal God was in the blood of the Lord Jesus as the Son of man. That is what made His blood precious. That life of His was offered for our redemption. The shedding of His blood was the pouring out of His blood as a sacrifice for sins. His cross was the theater of redeeming suffering—the place of atonement for the soul of man. We gaze with open eye upon His blood-stained cross, and know by divine certainty that He "purged our sins" (Heb. 1:3).

There every stain may be washed away. The blood of Christ does that! We must remember that in His body—a truly human body—Deity was also present with His Manhood. He is the Mighty God. His blood is the blood of God (Acts 20:28). If it were less, it could effect no redemption. This is the marrow of the gospel. Jesus is God. His blood is precious blood, and it is enough!

Also, His blood keeps on cleansing (1 Jn. 1:7). This continued efficacy is not a repetition of the sacrifice. Our Lord was "once offered." The offering of His body was "once for all" and He offered the one sacrifice "for ever." Calvary could never be repeated; never again could sacrifice be made for sins. Yet that sacrificial blood has permanent value. It keeps on cleansing forever, not intermittently. That blood dealt with sins once for all and forever.

PRECIOUS LORD

"He is precious" (1 Pet. 2:7). This is spoken in the context where we are told that He is so as the chief cornerstone of God's spiritual house. Solomon came to the throne of Israel for the supreme purpose of building the temple. On completion, God's glory filled the whole. It was the embodiment of the glory of God. The stones that Solomon used for the building were cut out of a deep quarry, and were shaped, chiseled, and polished to a divine pattern. Each had its God-appointed place, and all fitted perfectly together.

Thus it is in God's spiritual house. The Lord Jesus builds with living stones—men and women made alive to God by the new birth. He is the chief Cornerstone, joining Jew and Gentile, bond and free, male and female, circumcision and uncircumcision, Scythian and barbarian. To all who are part of that spiritual house of His, "He is precious." They are what they are, and where they are, through His great sacrifice on the cross.

The Lord Jesus is the truest treasure man can ever gain. He is the sweetest cordial which the lips of faith can drink. He is heaven's "sweet savor." There is none like our Lord—the altogether lovely One! All peace and joy, all happiness and holiness are in Him, and in Him alone. "He is precious." May we prize Him so.

Fairest Lord Jesus! Ruler of all nature!
O Thou, of God and man, the Son!
Thee will I cherish, Thee will I honor,
Thou my soul's glory, joy, and crown!

185

Fair is the sunshine, fairer still the moonlight,
And all the twinkling starry host;
Jesus shines brighter, Jesus shines purer
Than all the angels heaven can boast!

All fairest beauty, heavenly and earthly,
Wondrously, Jesus, is found in Thee;
None can be nearer, fairer, or dearer,
Than Thou my Saviour, art to me.

—CRUSADER'S HYMN

42
The Burnt Offering

It is a burnt sacrifice, an offering made by fire,
of a sweet savor unto the Lord.
LEVITICUS 1:17

The five offerings in the beginning of the book of Leviticus foreshadow the sacrifice of our Lord on Calvary's cross. In Exodus, we read of God's people groaning under bondage. In Leviticus, after redemption is effected, they become a worshiping people. Within a divinely patterned and erected tabernacle, they worship in God's appointed way. The golden key to these offerings is Christ in His grace and work. All the action honors God, and the burnt offering takes the lead.

THE SACRIFICE

There were degrees of devotion in what was offered. It could be a male from the herd, a sheep, or even a small bird. If the offering was from the herd (Lev. 1:3), it had to be an unblemished male, speaking of perfection and strength. It was choice and prime. It represented strength in fullest vigor and beauty in perfection. That was the highest degree of devotion.

The quality of the offering itself pointed to the suitability of the

Lord Jesus as the only acceptable offering to God. He must be God to satisfy the infinite heart of God. And if God was not satisfied with Christ, it would not matter whether we were satisfied with Him—there would be no acceptance for us with God without our being "accepted in the Beloved."

The offerer had to exercise his personal desire to present his offering. There was no compulsion. There was to be no reluctance. It was to be a willing offering. Here we see the free and happy offering of a devoted heart. Such a person knows sin's miserable burden. He also knows the value of redeeming love. There is nothing formal here, nothing cold and dead. Faith is a willing grace.

The offerer then put his hand on the offering's head (Lev. 1:4). This was an act of transference. This transfer was not the same as in the sin offerings when, figuratively, all his sin was placed on the head of his offering. In this case, the imputation was in the other direction—"it shall be accepted for him." In other words, the acceptability of the offering was accounted to the poor sinner who was willing to identify with the "perfect" sacrifice. In this way, we find our acceptance with God, not in our own merit, but in Christ's.

THE SACRIFICE SLAIN

"He shall kill the bullock before the Lord" (Lev. 1:5). That which would provide such acceptance, cannot be spared. Death alone can satisfy the God of heaven. It must be satisfaction for God by the Lord Jesus being obedient, even to the point of "the death of the cross." Thus we see clearly in this type how Christ must die so that Satan's accusations may be silenced. "If God be for us, who can be against us?" (Rom. 8:31).

The blood of the sacrifice was then sprinkled "round about upon the altar" (Lev. 1:5). This was a sprinkling of it over a wide area, and here we learn the wide use of the blood to gain all covenant blessings, and the full reward and fruit of the finished work.

The sacrifice was next flayed, or skinned (Lev. 1:6). The skin provided raiment for the offerer, which sets forth Christ our Lord as "the Lord our righteousness" through whose sacrifice we are clothed with the best robe heaven can provide, the pure robe of God's own righteousness given to the offerer as a free gift.

The limbs of the sacrifice were all separated and thoroughly washed (1:9). Jesus was *clean,* but that which stands as a type of Jesus must be *cleansed.* There must be no speck of impurity, for "[God] is of purer eyes than to behold evil." All the sacrifice, in all its parts, was then placed on the altar and the fire consumed it all to ashes (1:9).

The burning here is not the same word used for the offerings for sin. There it is *to utterly consume.* There the fire made the sin and trespass offerings disappear, so to speak. But in the sweet savor offerings, the word is *olah,* meaning *to cause to ascend.* Here the offering is turned into aroma and smoke by the fire, sending it heavenward to be received by God as a sweet smell, a fragrance of rest.

THE SACRIFICE SEALED

It is "a burnt sacrifice, an offering made by fire, of a sweet savor unto the Lord" (Lev. 1:9). This is the witness of God's Holy Spirit, written for the everlasting comfort of the redeemed. It is the witness of Heaven, the seal of God, the sweet assurance that the sacrifice of God's beloved Son is fully acceptable to God. It is "a sweet savor." Because God is satisfied, a ground is provided where we can rest as well. It gives Him a channel to communicate His peace and joy to the offerer. What wisdom! What love!

We should never come to the Lord's Supper without some solemn thought of what is sin's due. What a terrible end it must be to be without Christ, when He, the Son of God, had to suffer so. Yet we have not reached the highest plane in worship until we have passed the offerings for sin and appreciated the sweet savor aspects of the offering of Christ which bring pleasure to both God and man.

> *Lord, e'en to death Thy love could go,*
> *A death of shame and loss,*
> *To vanquish for us every foe,*
> *And break the strong man's force.*

189

O, what a load was Thine to bear,
Alone in that dark hour,
Our sins in all their terror there,
God's wrath and Satan's power!

The storm that bowed Thy blessed head,
Is hushed forever now,
And rest divine is ours instead,
While glory crowns Thy brow.

—H. L. ROSSIER
TR. BY MISS C. A. WELLESLEY

43
The Meal Offering

When any will offer a meat offering unto the Lord,
his offering shall be of fine flour.
Leviticus 2:1

The varied offerings are to show us different aspects of the Saviour's sacrifice in figure. Each offering is to illustrate the redemption which our Lord purchased for us. These ancient scriptures are a mine of wealth. They show more of Christ than what we can discern.

The meal offering is the second of the five. God's wisdom has termed it the "meat" or "food" offering.[1] This particular offering had a secondary use—to supply food for the priest.

The Substance of the Offering

The chief material was fine flour (Lev. 2:1). It is the infinite mind of God which selected the substance, so the thought is deep. And, may we ask, by what process is flour formed? It is formed from

---

1. Due to changes in the English language, the *meat* offering (KJV) is the only one of the five not of meat in the modern sense. It is sometimes called the food or meal offering, the meaning of the Hebrew word, *minchah.*

earth-grown grain which is threshed from the husk and ground in a mill to powder. Faith easily discerns in this the story of our Lord's life on earth. He was born into this arena. No blow was spared Him. He was buffeted with all the fury of men and devils, and even the justice of His own holy law crushed Him.

The flour was *fine* flour. There were no lumps, no vestiges of unevenness. This sets forth the Saviour's sinless character and the perfect evenness of His temperament. He is the perfect Man and, therefore, the perfect offering.

Oil was added (Lev. 2:1)—the blessed emblem in Scripture of the Holy Spirit's anointing. The Lord, we read, is given the Spirit "not...by measure" (Jn. 3:34). The Holy Spirit formed His body (Lk. 1:35), descended upon Him in baptism (Lk. 3:22), was with Him in His testings (Lk. 4:1), upheld Him on Calvary's cross (Heb. 9:14), and aided Him in breaking the bands of death (1 Pet. 3:18). The Lord Jesus was rich in the Spirit's anointing.

Frankincense was then sprinkled (Lev. 2:1). This was to give the offering a sweet fragrance. It spoke of Him whose name was "as ointment poured forth" (Song of Sol. 1:3). However, though man could enjoy the aroma, it is to be noted that while only a handful of the flour and oil was sacrificed, *all* the frankincense was placed on the altar. This suggests that the life of Christ was lived solely for the pleasure of God.

No leaven and no honey could be brought (Lev. 2:11). Leaven changes the meal and is an emblem of evil. Leaven spreads its influence throughout, and so is forbidden. Honey is natural sweetness, but ferments, and in this it expresses the natural sentiment that would have kept Him from the cross: "Be it far from Thee, Lord."

But salt was added (2:13). Salt repels corruption and arrests decay. It brought freshness and taste to the offering, and in this, too, we see blessed features of our Lord. His word is an everlasting covenant of salt, sealed with Himself as the Amen to all the promises of God (2 Cor. 1:20).

Thus, in every part of the substance of the meal offering we see Jesus our Lord portrayed in the precious character that He is. There is nothing more gladdening to the soul than the intrinsic perfection of His holy life. The meal offering is a mirror in which we see the absolute perfection of every virtue He reveals, apart from His death. In worship, we should not be so occupied with our blessings that we forget the Blesser Himself

THE USE OF THE OFFERING

The use is very clearly set forth. In the first place, it satisfied God. We see this in that part of the offering was to be burned on the altar "to be an offering made by fire, of a sweet savor unto the Lord" (2:2). The burning meal sets forth the Lord in the anguish, not of His death—for there is no blood here—but in the sufferings of His life. God "spared not His own Son," even on His way to the cross. But every step of His pathway brought the Father's approval: "This is My beloved Son in Whom I am well pleased."

Then, a second use of the offering was that it provided food. The remaining part "shall be Aaron's and his sons': it is a thing most holy of the offerings of the Lord made by fire" (Lev. 2:3). It shows Christ as the Provider for His people, the true Bread of life for hungry souls. Christ in His life is the substantial and satisfying food for all who believe. "My flesh is meat indeed, and My blood is drink indeed" (Jn. 6:55). "Eat, O friends; drink, yea, drink abundantly, O beloved," says Song of Solomon 5:1. And faith brings the hungry to the banqueting table. Faith partakes of Christ and feasts upon Him. There is no other way to gain strength for the journey heavenwards. The soul must feed on Christ if it would endure all the way.

As we saw in the burnt offering, so here in the meal offering there are diverse ways of preparing the offering. With some it was baked in an oven; with others, in a pan; with still others, in a frying pan. All such things have infinite and profound meaning. Some of Christ's sufferings in life were open to view; some were seen by only a few; some were hidden to all but God.

At the practical level, the variety of preparation showed that from the richest to the poorest could come with this offering. There is no other Christ to offer. Bring this offering of Christ to God and, no mat-

193

ter what your station in life, you will be accepted by Him, and you will be fully fed and satisfied.

What food luxurious loads the board
When, at His table, sits the Lord!
The wine how rich, the bread how sweet,
When Jesus deigns His guests to meet!

If now, with eyes defiled and dim,
We see the signs, but see not Him;
O, may His love the scales displace,
And bid us see Him face to face!

Thou glorious Bridegroom of our hearts,
Thy present smile a heaven imparts!
O, lift the veil, if veil there be,
Let every saint Thy glory see!

—CHARLES H. SPURGEON

44
The Peace Offering

A sacrifice of peace offering.
Leviticus 3:1

Peace is what mankind has always sought; but peace can be found only in the Lord Jesus Christ. Peace was announced by His coming. Declared the angels at His birth, "On earth peace." Sin brought in enmity, but the scheme by which peace could be replanted in the heart of man was modeled in the ancient peace offering.

The Mark of the Offering

The offering could be a male or female and taken from cattle, sheep, or goats (Lev. 3:1, 6, 12). This made the offering possible to all classes[1] and so readily at hand. No man would have to search very

---

1. There was one limitation. In this offering, unlike the other animal sacrifices, no birds were allowed—the offering of the very poor. God, having received the animals, then gave them back to the people, spreading a feast for them. There would not be much left of a pigeon or dove once the feathers, skin, blood, fat, breast, and "shoulder" were removed, and God would never serve up a skimpy feast.

far for such an offering. And so readily obtainable is our blessed Saviour—always at hand. He is never beyond the reach of any.

The offering, since it was a model of Christ, was to be free from fault. Any fault would have debarred Christ our Lord from being an acceptable offering to a holy God. Only a sinless offering could make a sufficient sacrifice for others. Had there been sin in the Lord Jesus Himself, then He would have been forced to make sacrifice for Himself and we would have no Saviour.

The offerer placed his hands on his offering as well. The peace or reconciliation offering—the middle offering—was to be the place of meeting between God and man. Thus the offerer accepted the ground of peace: God's provision in His Son "for He is our peace."

The appointed offering was then slain (Lev. 3:2). Death is the God-appointed desert of sin, but now through grace we see how it falls on Christ our Lord, as here in the model. This was the price of peace—the only means by which peace could be restored.

THE DIVISION OF THE OFFERING

The offering was divided into three parts. First, there was a part for God. This was the choicest part of the offering: the fat or energy of the offering, speaking of the motivation of Christ that took Him to the cross; the blood, or life of the offering, speaking of the price He was willing to pay to procure peace; and the inwards, illustrating the hidden thoughts and motives of His Son, all sweet to God.

This was placed on the altar and was sent heavenward by fire (Lev. 3:3-5). Thus the first part is brought to God, and in it God smelled the savor of rest, finding the place where He could righteously meet with man, reconciling sinners to Himself in Christ.

Secondly, provision was made for those who serve. The Lord is never debtor to any man; they who leave all for Him in order to do Him service, have the needs of their own souls fully met. Their food is the same as that which satisfies God. Let all who serve know that their spiritual strength for service is through Christ as their peace offering. They cannot labor unless they feed on the Lord. This alone can produce the energy which will never flag, and gird the loins with sufficient strength for every demanding duty.

Thirdly, the offerer took his portion. The essence of true faith lies in the partaking of our Lord—the inward receiving of Him. It is not mental knowledge, the outward handling of truth, which brings peace. It is feeding by faith on Christ as our offering of peace. Here warning is given by the Lord that the unclean may not partake (Lev. 7:20). Impurity will never lead to peace with God. God has provided means for the cleansing away of all sin, but neglect of such means cannot bring about such a gracious end. They who sit down without a wedding garment are cast out (Mt. 22:13). "There is no peace, saith the Lord, unto the wicked" (Isa. 48:22).

THE MOTIVE OF THE OFFERER

The offerer was first prompted by a sense of gratitude. His debts had been large, but now have been paid. His substitute has paid to the full. This then prompted another exercise: the offerer vowed and made a pledge to live for God (Lev. 7:12, 16). These two resolutions were fair flowers which now began to bloom in the life of the offerer after peace had been made.

The heart of those who have experienced such peace should always be full, and flowing forth in ceaseless praise. Who could count the number of God's mercies? Who could withhold his songs of praise? But should not gratitude lead to dedication, and to a purposeful resolve of heart to devote one's life to the service of such a Saviour?

But none can praise, and none can serve, until peace is made with God. Such praise can rise, and such service can be given, only where peace abounds. These great exercises of the soul were to be done without delay. "It shall be eaten the same day that he offereth his sacrifice." No remnant left to the third day was to be touched (Lev. 7:16-17). There was to be no delay, no vacillation, no lingering, no reluctance. So with us today. The Lord Jesus has spread the feast. He bids us sit down with instant joy. It is ours to partake without a moment's hesitation. The feast is set "to guide our feet into the way of peace."

197

Oh, the peace forever flowing
From God's thoughts of His own Son!
Oh, the peace of simply knowing
On the cross that all was done.

Peace with God! the blood in heaven
Speaks of pardon now to me:
Peace with God! the Lord is risen!
Righteousness now counts me free.

Peace with God is Christ in glory;
God is just and God is love;
Jesus died to tell the story,
Foes to bring to God above.

—A. P. CECIL

45

The Sin Offering

Let him bring for his sin, which he hath sinned, a young bullock without blemish unto the Lord for a sin offering.
LEVITICUS 4:3

Sin is a word with an ominous sound. The word is one of the briefest, but the thing itself dragged angels down from heaven and ruined our God-created humanity. Our Lord's cross flung a new and divine light upon sin as the abominable thing which God hates. There was sin on the earth before the Christ of God died, but it was imperfectly known.

Sin is no trifle with God; it is something He could not overlook. It is something at which God pointed His finger and said in effect, "I hate that, and that, and that." It marred the beauty of His creation. It brought forth weeds and thorns, and spawned natural calamity. It wrecked a beauteous world.

Sin was man's ruin. It drove man out of peaceful fellowship with God. It made him a hardened rebel. It brought his mind into total spiritual darkness, his affections into a nest of unclean birds, his will into a den of God-defying schemes. Worst of all, it was the mother of death. It has dug every grave since the world began, and filled the homes of earth's inhabitants with grief and sorrow. But it reaches beyond death and has built the prison house of hell, where all is eternal woe. God's curse is upon it.

The sin offering of Israel is designed to teach us the horrors of sin, and the terrible cost of expiation, but to display also the wonders of redeeming grace. The ancient rite in Israel's law shows the way of escape. The dire consequences of sin need not fall upon the sinner's head. There is a solution to the dread penalty. Its stain can be cleansed away. The debt may be forgiven.

THE GOOD TIDINGS

Justice and holiness in God demand that each sin bear a merited punishment. Each violation of law must drink the condemnation. With such strong demands from law, the Son of God comes forth from heaven to save us by meeting the stern terms. He takes the place of the guilty. He stands forth as the representative of His people. He assumes responsibility for all their sins. He suffers for each and all iniquity. Only because He is God can He absorb so much punishment.

But He is the complete sin offering. He pays with His own precious blood. He endures the full and awful wrath of God against the sin of man. His manhood qualifies Him to do this, and His deity upholds Him. It is thus that sin is fully punished, and the redeemed are fully saved. All who believe, live and walk in freedom from sin.

THE OFFENDER AND HIS SACRIFICE

There are differences in men. The first offender here is the priest himself—to teach us that the very holiest of men are sinners, and that none can approach God without an adequate sin offering. Sin has allured, and snared, and defiled the best of men. Even the priest in Israel's ancient ceremonials must see his own guilt and his need for pardon. Thus he must bring an unblemished young bullock to the tabernacle door. This is a God-given direction, and the offering is a God-chosen one.

God Himself has decreed the plan of redemption. He willed the ransom, and His Son achieved it through the Spirit's aid. The sin offering of Israel speaks of the Saviour to come, and clearly shows how atonement is provided by Him.

The offender's hands must be placed on the victim's head. This is the transmission of his guilt. The sin of the offender thus passes to the sin offering. Here we are instructed how to roll our sins upon Christ as our Sin-Bearer. The wages of sin is death; the soul that sins must die. Sin and its penalties are absolute certainties. Whoever bears sin must hear judicial doom before the righteous Judge. If God's beloved Son bears our sins, then there can be for Him no mitigation of the punishment. God cannot lower His demands, nor abate any of His wrath against sin, even in the case of His own Son acting as Substitute.

THE USES OF THE BLOOD

The first use of blood is that the veil is sprinkled seven times (Lev. 4:6). The veil hung before the mercy seat and was the entrance into the holiest of all. This sprinkling means that those who would pass into God's immediate presence—into His holy heaven—must be blood-sprinkled. There can be no coming to God without the remedy of sin-removing blood.

Secondly, the blood was put on the horns of the golden altar (4:7). This was the place from which sweet incense arose, emblem of ascending prayer. Our Lord's intercession for us prevails because of His shed blood. The blood of Jesus is our strength in its supplication. Nothing can ascend to God, most holy, until it is washed clean from all pollutants. What we are and have must be washed by His blood.

Thirdly, the remainder of the blood was poured out at the bottom of the brazen altar (4:7). Thus all is used to bring assurance to the heart. Each drop of blood has its value. Our atonement needs the whole of our Lord's sacrifice—all His blood—and the whole is freely given.

THE SHAME HEAPED ON THE OFFERING

When the costliest parts were burnt on the altar, we see more than substitutionary death. The sin offering had to be an accursed thing.

201

So then, the remnant of the victim was borne outside the camp and was consumed with fire. This is a picture of Christ made a curse for us (Gal. 3:13; Heb. 13:11). He is cast out as earth's refuse. The curse falls on the Saviour's cross—"made a curse"—how shocking! What a price for Him to pay!

Alas! and did my Saviour bleed?
And did my Sovereign die?
Would He devote that sacred head
For such a worm as I?

Was it for crimes that I have done
He groaned upon the tree?
Amazing pity! grace unknown!
And love beyond degree!

Thus might I hide my blushing face,
While His dear cross appears;
Dissolve my heart in thankfulness,
And melt my eyes to tears.

—ISAAC WATTS

46

The Trespass Offering

If a soul commit a trespass, and sin through ignorance,
in the holy things of the Lord; then he shall bring for his trespass
unto the Lord a ram without blemish out of the flocks,
with thy estimation by shekels of silver, after the shekel
of the sanctuary, for a trespass offering.
And he shall make amends for the harm that he hath done
in the holy thing, and shall add the fifth part thereto,
and give it unto the priest: and the priest shall make an atonement
for him with the ram of the trespass offering,
and it shall be forgiven him.
LEVITICUS 5:15-16

THE SUBSTITUTE

Sin has many forms, and everything it touches it wounds and imparts death. These verses state the first case of the trespass offering. It is the case of a soul sinning through ignorance. God's law has been infringed, and His holy will set at nought. But, though done in ignorance, it is no trifle with God. That sin can never be. Every form of iniquity is hated by God. God's throne would lose its pristine whiteness if any sin were condoned.

THE OFFENSE

This rite especially condemns transgression in holy things. What would such transgression be? It could be trying to be righteous by one's own merits. It is Cain religion—bringing to God the fruit of one's own toil—choosing the rags of our own righteousness, rather than the gospel robe of God's free gift of righteousness. This trespass has a fair exterior, but it slays the soul.

There is much of it in our world. All human religions invented by man are typical of sins of trespass in holy things—religions such as Hinduism, Islam, Buddhism, Confucianism, and all cults which deny the Godhood of the Lord Jesus and His finished atoning work at Calvary. Devotees of such will not take up God's plan, and they refuse to be taught the way of God. They invent their own way.

But, again, the trespass can be seen in those who know the truth of God, but bring to Him no more than the ceremonial round, the regular attendance, a fair contribution of money, the faithful adherence to the church creed—as if sufficient to secure the crown of life. So many believe, alas, to their ruin.

Both these ways lead to woe. They are simply opposing falsehoods. Both are Satan's delusion. Such trespasses live only in dens of ignorance. But though spawned in ignorance, they are still trespasses and bring the demand of full payment.

Once again we see the dying victim as the prototype proclaiming Christ the Lord. He is the trespass offering. He is "made...sin for us." He suffers all our deserved punishment. He drinks up all our woe.

This amazing grace is the eternal song of the saved, the "joy unspeakable and full of glory." This is the hope set before us, which is as an anchor of the soul, sure and steadfast. The trespass offering bleeds and dies, and only by such substitution can the offender be forgiven. So Jesus dies, and all His family of believing people are saved. And "Who shall lay any thing to the charge of God's elect? It is God that justifieth. Who is he that condemneth? It is Christ that died, yea rather, that is risen again, who is even at the right hand of God, who also maketh intercession for us" (Rom. 8:33-34).

THE REPAYMENT

The need of sinful man is vast. None can measure the dimensions of guilt's trespass, but the work of our Lord covers it all. Here we see that the value of the trespass must be reckoned. The cost must be paid according to the sanctuary's weight—not what man feels is the value. Thus here in this ancient rite we see a fifth part added. It is not enough to give equal. There must be excess (Lev. 5:16).

Why is this? Because trespass defrauds God. Sin is not only an offense against a law but a defrauding of God. Nothing we have is our own. Everything, therefore, which God has given us should be used to do Him honor and augment His praise. But we have robbed God of this! It would be vain conceit, too, to imagine we could make it up to Him. The debt is huge, and only God's beloved Son can pay it. No devotedness can repay. Surplus of merit is but a papist's dream. All our works only increase our debt, only deepen our bankruptcy.

Thus the trespass offerer added a surplus. Where sin abounded, grace super-abounded. Who can measure the surplus which the Lord Jesus brought to Calvary's cross? In that cross is all that God can give—and all that God can take. This makes the offering of Christ so full, so precious and divine.

Let us acknowledge before God that trespass stains our hearts, that we do often trespass even in holy things. Let us also remember that this form of trespass is as offensive to God as vulgar sin. It raises the same barrier between the soul and God. But here in the trespass offering, the Lord Jesus is depicted again in the brightest hues. He died to pay the trespass offering. Only as we cling to Him can our trespass be forgiven. His cross is the only expiation for every sin, as well as for the damage that sin has done. His surplus payment is more than enough.

> *Worthy of homage and of praise;*
> *Worthy by all to be adored:*
> *Exhaustless theme of heavenly lays!*
> *Thou, Thou art worthy, Jesus, Lord.*

205

To Thee, e'en now, our song we raise,
Tho' sure the tribute mean must prove:
No mortal tongue can tell Thy ways,
So full of light and life and love.

Yet, Saviour, Thou shalt have full praise:
We soon shall meet Thee in the cloud,
We soon shall see Thee face to face,
In glory praising as we would.

—Miss F. T. Wigram

47

The Resurrection Side of the Cross

He must go unto Jerusalem, and suffer many things...and be killed, and be raised again the third day.

MATTHEW 16:21

The emphasis of the New Testament is on the death of the Lord Jesus, since by His death He dealt with our sins and wrought out redemption for us. He took them far away—so far away that God cannot find them!

When the Saviour died, life seemed to be extinct. The grave made fast its bars. But every foe was foiled. Death and hell yielded. The tomb opened its portal. The mighty Conqueror strode forth alive. He was the firstfruits from among the dead.

THE RESURRECTION DEMONSTRATES HIS DEITY

Christ was "declared to be the Son of God with power, according to the spirit of holiness, by the resurrection from the dead" (Rom. 1:4). When our Lord warned His disciples that He must die, they did not understand it. Was He really the Son of God? When at last He was arrested, tried, condemned, and crucified, the disciples were dev-

207

astated. Instead of reigning over a kingdom on earth, as they supposed He would, He had suffered the shame and ignominy of crucifixion. How could He be the Son of God and allow men to kill Him? Might it be that He was not the Messiah, the Redeemer? So they may have queried.

But then He arose; He lives; He comes forth again to ascend to the Father. And in His resurrection He was powerfully declared to be the Son of God. The resurrection proved it beyond a shadow of doubt.

A very important event in the Old Testament was the ejecting of Jonah by the great fish which had swallowed him. This was a pointer to our Lord's resurrection, a sign of this momentous event.

It was the resurrection which convinced Mary in the garden, which restored Peter's confidence after his threefold denial, which made Thomas cry, "My Lord and my God," which revived the hopes of the two despondent disciples who were going to Emmaus, which brought new hope to those who had gone back fishing and had caught nothing, and which convinced Saul of Tarsus on the Damascus Road.

THE RESURRECTION CONFIRMS THE EFFICACY OF HIS DEATH

"We believe on Him that raised up Jesus our Lord from the dead; who was delivered for our offenses, and was raised again for our justification" (Rom. 4:24-25). When the Lord Jesus died, anxious hearts may have inquired: He came, He died to save us; but how can we be sure He succeeded?

The Lord Himself had foretold not only His death but the purpose of it: "to give His life a ransom for many," that His blood was to be shed for the remission of sins. But how do we know that for sure? May He not have failed?

Oh, no! The resurrection proves that the purpose for which He died was accomplished. All claims were satisfied. All enemies were subdued. All the worst that hell could do against Him was now a spent wind. The resurrection was God's evidence that our Lord had not died in vain. Because that purpose had been accomplished, and full satisfaction for sins had been made, God raised Him from the dead for our justification. The Apostle Paul in 1 Corinthians 15:17-18, 20, says, "If Christ be not raised, your faith is vain; ye are yet in your sins. Then they also which are fallen asleep in Christ are perished...But now is Christ risen from the dead, and become the first-fruits of them that slept." So believers are no longer in their sins, but are justified from all things. Those who have died in the Lord have not perished, but are safe home with the Lord.

THE RESURRECTION COMPLETES HIS REDEMPTIVE WORK

"For if we have been planted together in the likeness of His death, we shall be also in the likeness of His resurrection" (Rom. 6:5). The resurrection of our body is part of redemption's fruit. Death, like the devil, is a conquered foe. It will come and extend its hand to take down our crumbling clay abodes. It will consign the bodies of believers to a narrow cell, and worms will do their work. This body is sin-soiled and cannot be taken into God's heaven as it is anyway.

But death's seeming triumph over the body is a real defeat. It wounds only to heal. It means that the body will rise in fresher beauty. Oh, how changed that body will be! It shall shine brighter than the noonday sun. It will no longer be subject to natural laws but liberated to soar in the spiritual realms.

We can hardly conceive the glory of that resurrection body. But it is true—and it is near. The trumpet will soon sound to call the bodies of believers to arise. The Lord of life is at the door. This is part of the blessed gospel, that we glory in resurrection hope.

Then will the Lord display before the Father the many members who compose His spiritual body. He pleads that they may be gathered from the world. He offers them as consecrated for the Father's use. What a sight that will be! To see the Saviour's nail-marked hand present our fully redeemed persons to God the Father!

One day they led Him up Calvary's mountain,
One day they nailed Him to die on the tree;
Suffering anguish, despised and rejected:
Bearing our sins, my Redeemer is He.

209

One day the grave could conceal Him no longer,
One day the stone rolled away from the door;
Then He arose, over death He had conquered;
Now is ascended, my Lord evermore!

One day the trumpet will sound for His coming,
One day the skies with His glories will shine;
Wonderful day, my beloved ones bringing;
Glorious Saviour, this Jesus is mine!

—J. WILBUR CHAPMAN

48

Our Lord's Place in Heaven

He was taken up, and a cloud received Him out of their sight.
ACTS 1:9

Our Lord's ascension into heaven was a historical event. He went up in His resurrection body, having been raised from the dead. His ascension was actual, physical, historical, visible, and in the presence of His disciples. We read that He was "received up" (Mk. 16:19); "carried up" (Lk. 24:51); "taken up" (Acts 1:9); and that He, by His own power, went up (Eph. 4:9). We are told that "a cloud received Him." Had there been no clouds then He would have become smaller and smaller in His ascent, and this the Father does not allow His Son to become to us.

THE SEVEN STAGES OF HIS ASCENSION

1. Hebrews 4:14. "A great high priest, that is passed into [through] the heavens." This refers to the visible heavens. In the tabernacle of old, the Jewish high priests passed first from the altar through the outer court, which answers to the visible heavens.

2. Ephesians 1:21. "Far above all." So we are told of His ascension. This means far beyond and infinitely higher than all created intelligences.

3. Hebrews 9:24. "Christ is not entered into the holy places made with hands...but into heaven itself." This is entrance into the realm above the, air, clouds, sun, moon, and stars, into the realm of God's actual abode, where He reigns on the throne of all the universe.

4. Hebrews 8:1-2. "An high priest...of the sanctuary." This sanctuary answers to the holy place in the earthly tabernacle, a kind of second heaven which in the tabernacle was entered through a veil, and where Jewish high priests served the table, the lampstand, and the incense altar. These ministries, in their spiritual form, our Lord now has taken up as the High Priest of His redeemed people—a sparkling evidence that He can relieve soul hunger, chase all dark gloom away, and perfume all our sacrifices of praise with His own adorable merits.

5. Hebrews 6:19-20. "...Within the veil; whither the Forerunner is for us entered, even Jesus." This would answer to the Jewish high priests' entrance into the holy of holies, though they did not do so as forerunners. Our Lord entered within the veil that He might sprinkle before the mercy seat His own blood of everlasting efficacy, and guarantee our following Him into the Father's real presence.

6. Hebrews 8:1. "Who is set on the right hand of the throne of the Majesty in the heavens." This is the essence and crown of His function as our High Priest, for it demonstrates His excellent dignity. The words ascribe to the Lord Jesus equality with the Father, combined with His office of priestly administration. He, like Melchizedek, is a Priest upon His throne.

7. Hebrews 9:24. "To appear in the presence of God for us." These words may read: "to appear face to face with God for us." He turns, as it were, to unashamedly look full into the face of His holy Father and, as the Son of Man, be assured of the efficacy of His intercessions on our behalf. He carries a full receipt in His pierced hands for our everlasting acceptance.

THE FOUR ATTITUDES OF OUR LORD IN HEAVEN

1. Sitting: "He was received up into heaven, and sat on the right hand of God" (Mk. 16:19). It is significant that it is Mark, whose

Gospel emphasizes our Lord in His earthly toil, who tells us of our Lord *sitting* in the heavenly place. This indicates the end of His toil, the completion of His earthly work.

In Hebrews 1:3, we are told that He, "when He had by Himself purged our sins, sat down on the right hand of the Majesty on high." His sitting, in this instance, indicated the end of the purging of our sins, the completion of redemption.

In Hebrews 10:12, we read, "This man, after He had offered one sacrifice for sins for ever, sat down on the right hand of God." The emphasis here is on the words "for ever." The Lord did not have to rise to repeat redemption's work. It was finished forever.

2. Standing: There are two references to His standing. The first is in Acts 7:55, when He stood in heaven at the martyrdom of Stephen. It would appear as though He graciously went over, as it were, to personally welcome His martyred servant home.

In Revelation 5:6, we read that "in the midst of the throne...stood a Lamb as it had been slain." Here we see Him rise to pour out the final judgments of God on a godless world, to wind up all the kingdoms of darkness and establish His own glorious kingdom on this very earth where He was crucified.

3. Ministering: Hebrews 8:2 tells of His serving. In the days of His flesh, our Lord spoke of being "among you as He that serveth." He continued in this lowly office, even in His triumphal resurrection days (Jn. 21:13). Now in glory it is still His delight to serve His people, ministering to their needs from the true tabernacle in heaven.

4. Waiting: He waits, first, until all His enemies are put under His feet (1 Cor. 15:25). But also He waits for His elect bride, the Church, and for that blessed day when He shall receive her into His arms of loving embrace (Jn. 14:3). We often think of ourselves as the waiting ones. But our Lord waits, too, and that with great eager anticipation to receive the bride whom He has won to Himself with so great a measure of struggle and anguish.

Oh, what love! How marvelous is the love which exists in this union of Christ and His Church. How bright our future when we shall be Home in His prepared place for all the ages of eternity!

213

Golden harps are sounding,
Angel voices ring,
Pearly gates are opened,
Opened for the King:
Christ the King of Glory,
Jesus, King of Love,
Is gone up in triumph
To His throne above.

He who came to save us,
He who bled and died,
Now is crowned with glory
At His Father's side:
Never more to suffer,
Never more to die,
Jesus, King of Glory,
Is gone up on high.

Praying for His children
In that blessed place,
Calling them to glory,
Sending them His grace:
His bright Home preparing,
Faithful ones, for you;
Jesus ever liveth,
Ever loveth, too.

—FRANCES RIDLEY HAVERGAL

49
Where, When, How

True worshipers shall worship the Father in spirit and in truth.
JOHN 4:23

The first meeting place between God and man, after man's ruin by sin, was at an altar of sacrifice. Later on came God's desire for a sanctuary that He might dwell among His people, so the tabernacle was built. Still later, God gave instructions for the more permanent temple which Solomon built. In the New Testament, and with the Lord's coming into our humanity, our Lord spoke of His own body as the true temple. Then, later, believers were "builded together" into a holy, spiritual temple, that from their redeemed hearts there would arise worship.

God has often lost the worship He deserves through the ruin of sin. The whole plan of redemption was to restore men to be true worshipers. God asks and seeks for the worship of His creatures. It was about worship that the Lord spoke to the woman of Samaria. Since she was such a profligate person, we would have thought it more appropriate to have spoken to her about the new birth. Why speak of worship to such a sinner as she was? Because it was in the matter of worship that the Samaritans had gone far astray, and because the first inquiry of the woman had to do with that subject.

215

So to this poor sinful woman our Lord spoke of the Father, that the hour was come to worship Him in spirit and in truth. He then added these remarkable words: "The Father seeketh such to worship Him." What our Lord was emphasizing to this woman was the difference between the outward and the inward exercise, between the unreal and the real, between the unacceptable and the acceptable.

Samaria and Jerusalem, with their mounts Gerizim and Moriah, were external places where Samaritans and Jews worshiped. But God is not the God of the outward, not the God of places, but of living beings. He is not the God of cities and mountains, but of the hearts and souls of men. No sites or buildings, however ornate and beautiful, can substitute for the worship of the spirit. The matter of worship is neither intellectual nor aesthetic, but something essentially spiritual. Worship is not what gratifies the senses or what is tasteful to the ear and eye, but what is acceptable to God.

WHERE AM I TO WORSHIP?

Man asks that question, and answers it in his own way. So often men have chosen a certain sacred spot where a godly man has lived, and consecrated such places by sacred rites. But God's answer to "Where?" is "everywhere"—on sea or land, in vale or hill, in desert or garden, on moor or fen—anywhere and everywhere.

WHEN AM I TO WORSHIP?

Man answers this query in his own way, as well. His answer is: at certain times, certain hours, certain days, and these often arranged by priestly authority, or by ecclesiastical law, or by traditional rule. But God's answer is at all times and in all seasons. The naming of days and hours is indeed necessary for public gatherings for worship, but worship itself is to be perpetual, without the restraints of time. All hours are holy. All days are holy. One day may be set aside for corporate gathering, but only because of order and not for restriction.

HOW AM I TO WORSHIP?

Man asks the question and again answers in his own way. He may

216

say: in certain ornate buildings, a pillared cathedral with ceremonies, vestments, processions, and postures. But all such performances are the will-worship of man's self-righteousness. By these performances man distorts worship; he misrepresents God; he indulges his own sensuous taste.

But God's answer is clearly given by His Son to the woman at the well: "They that worship Him must worship Him in spirit and in truth." They may be in very poor garments; it matters not a thing. Knees may not be bent; there may be no consecrated building. These things are nothing to God. True worship is in, and from, the inner man. All else is of little consequence.

> *Father! Thy sovereign love has sought*
> *Captives to sin, gone far from Thee:*
> *The work that Thine own Son hath wrought*
> *Has brought us back, in peace, and free!*
> *And now, as sons before Thy face,*
> *With joyful steps the path we tread*
> *Which leads us on to that blest place*
> *Prepared for us by Christ, our Head!*
>
> *Thou gav'st us in eternal love*
> *To Christ, to bring us home to Thee,*
> *Suited to Thine own thoughts above*
> *As sons, like Him, with Him to be!*
> *O glorious grace that fills with joy*
> *Unmingled, all that enter there*
> *God's nature, love without alloy*
> *Our hearts are given e'en now to share!*
>
> *God's righteousness with glory bright,*
> *Which fills with radiance all that sphere*
> *E'en Christ—of God, the Power and Light—*
> *Our title is that Light to share!*

O Mind Divine! so must it be:
That glory all belongs to God!
O Love Divine! that did decree
Our part with Thee, through Jesus' blood.

—J. N. DARBY

50
The Lord's Sufferings Predicted

All things must be fulfilled, which were written in the law of Moses,
and in the prophets, and in the psalms, concerning Me.
LUKE 24:44

Since the sacrifice of God's Son was settled in the councils of the
Godhead before the world began, the Old Testament is full of predictions of it. In the above words, the risen Lord is simply confirm-
ing His own teaching during His earthly ministry. Nothing which the
Lord ever said had to be corrected or modified or changed. But He
did have to open the minds of His disciples to understand Old
Testament prediction (Lk. 24:45).

The sufferings and death of the Lord Jesus should not have taken
the disciples by surprise since they were somewhat familiar with Old
Testament scriptures. Indeed, they should have *expected* His passion.
The pages of the Old Testament sparkle with the jewels of predicted
redemption. They stand as a rich tree laden with the promises of God
regarding it. We can stand there as on a God-given height of revelation, and from it view all that our Lord was to suffer.

The Lord Jesus is the theme of all Scripture. He is the luster of
every page. To read the Old Testament aright is a sunlight walk with
Him. To read it aright surely opens redemption's plan. But the Jews

did not read the Old Testament rightly. They read of His coming kingdom and glory, and understood that! They understood, for instance, Daniel 7:14, "And there was given Him dominion, and glory, and a kingdom, that all people, nations, and languages, should serve Him: His dominion is an everlasting dominion, which shall not pass away, and His kingdom that which shall not be destroyed."

They expected that! But they were blind to the Lord's humiliation, as in Isaiah 53:5, "He was wounded for our transgressions, He was bruised for our iniquities: the chastisement of our peace was upon Him; and with His stripes we are healed." They could not see it.

After His resurrection, the Lord stressed this point: "All things must be fulfilled." There was a Saviour to be given; thus a Saviour to be born; a Saviour who would make adequate sacrifice for sins, the only sacrifice that God would ever accept and call men to bring; a sacrifice that God would never refuse. Thus the sufferings and death of the Lord Jesus are never spoken of in Scripture as a tragic mistake or an unforeseen accident. It was all God's own wise plan to rescue man from Satan's power, and it is all so clearly spelled out in the Old Testament.

True, there was man's side to the cross. Psalm 22 tells us that He would be compassed about with "bulls," the Jewish rulers; "dogs," the Gentile forces of Rome; "lions," the ferocious hosts of hell. There, too, is depicted man's ribald mockery, derisive laughter, universal scorn. But behind all this there is "the determinate counsel and foreknowledge of God" (Acts 2:23). The crucifying of Christ expresses all the inherent hatred in man's heart against God. But the purposeful laying down of His life was the manifestation of God's utter and complete love for fallen man. There was a divine necessity for the cross; God had no other way of dealing with human sin. It was clear from the beginning.

OLD TESTAMENT PREDICTIONS SPOKEN BY OUR LORD

When at Caesarea, our Lord said that "He must go unto Jerusalem, and suffer many things of the elders and chief priests and scribes, and be killed" (Mt. 16:21). Then, in Mark 9:12, He said, "It is written of the Son of man, that He must suffer many things, and be set at nought." Again, in Luke 18:31, "Behold, we go up to Jerusalem, and all things that are written by the prophets concerning the Son of man shall be accomplished."

Also, when Peter tried to stand in the way for our Lord's defense in the garden of Gethsemane, Jesus rebuked him with the words: "Put up...thy sword into his place...How then shall the scriptures be fulfilled, that thus it must be?" (Mt. 26:52, 54) In His walk to Emmaus with the two journeying there in post-resurrection days, the Lord Jesus said, "O fools, and slow of heart to believe all that the prophets have spoken: Ought not Christ to have suffered these things, and to enter into His glory?" (Lk. 24:25-26)

Thus the Saviour's sacrifice was written in letters of gold in the Old Testament. God's redemption plan shines forth telling the story that God's beloved Son would come and bear the sinner's sins. All such scriptures spring from the eternal Spirit of God, and display the sacrifice of God the Son in skillfully constructed symbols and forms.

OLD TESTAMENT PREDICTIONS BY THE APOSTLES

Look at Peter's declaration in Acts 3:18, "But those things, which God before had showed by the mouth of all His prophets, that Christ should suffer, He hath so fulfilled." When Paul is chosen and appointed, there is this remarkable statement by him in Acts 13:27, "For they that dwell at Jerusalem, and their rulers, because they knew Him not, nor yet the voices of the prophets which are read every sabbath day, they have fulfilled them in condemning Him."

Do we fully understand what that means? It means that the Old Testament books were read in synagogues every sabbath through centuries of time. The prophets cried of a death which would save from death, of a stream of blood which would cleanse away all sin, of a Messiah who would shelter them, hide them, and redeem them.

But they did not get the message! When He came to earth, their vile corruptions raised their heads. Unbelief blinded them. So they "killed the Prince of life" and, in doing so, fulfilled what the prophets said they would do: pierce His hands and feet, and make Him a curse

221

by hanging Him on a tree. It was all written—even the minutest detail of His sufferings and death—in the pages and predictions of the Old Testament.

Now I have found the ground wherein
Sure my soul's anchor may remain;
The wounds of Jesus for my sin,
Before the world's foundation slain;
Whose mercy shall unshaken stay,
When heaven and earth are fled away.

O Love, Thou bottomless abyss,
My sins are swallowed up in Thee;
Covered is my unrighteousness,
Nor spot of guilt remains on me;
While Jesus' blood, through earth and skies,
Mercy, free, boundless mercy, cries.

—CHARLES WESLEY

51

The Star and the Scepter

There shall come a Star out of Jacob,
and a Scepter shall rise out of Israel.
NUMBERS 24:17

One of the strangest characters in the Bible is Balaam. He is made to speak some of the sweetest prophecies concerning the coming of the Lord's Messiah, but these things did not come from his heart, nor did they rise from spiritual affections. In this man we see some of the deep workings of the human soul—how a person can be affected by the Word of God and the happiness of God's people, yet still take the downward road to hell's dark pit.

BALAAM'S HIRE

The hire of Balaam came about by the distress of Balak, king of Moab, over the constant conquests of Israel. Balaam was a Mesopotamian soothsayer who, living in close proximity to Israel, had learned to speak their spiritual language about God. He thus could wear a holy guise over a graceless heart. At first be gives the impression of really wanting to know God's mind. God's answer to his seeking is clear and plain: "Thou shalt not go with them: thou shalt not curse the people: for they are blessed" (22:12). But he does

223

not dismiss the representatives from the king of Moab. They return again and again, and both Balaam and the princes lessen the effect of each other's words until God is left out of the deal.

Balaam's eye is on the costly bribes of Balak. When he rises early to go with the men, a dumb ass is made to speak to block his way: "The dumb ass speaking with man's voice forbad the madness of the prophet" (2 Pet. 2:16). But the love of reward drives him on. So the tale goes on until both Balaam and Balak are thwarted. God put words into Balaam's mouth which are some of the sweetest words concerning the coming Messiah, and thus Christ is set forth even by a soul dead in his sins and most certainly an instrument of unrighteousness. But God makes him a vessel of dishonor to speak His truth.

THE STAR O F JACOB

"I shall see Him, but not now: I shall behold Him, but not nigh: there shall come a Star out of Jacob." Could any word of prophecy be more sweet and comforting? Could any statement glow with greater brightness? It means that in the background this world is sunk in darkness, heathenish gloom. All is the blackness of a godless world, a world in which all the excellencies and beauties of God's character are utterly unknown, and where the realities of His grace and love and truth are unseen. It is a jungle world where, because of the darkness, evil beasts creep abroad and prowl to vex the sons of men, tearing them to pieces. It is a world black with spots, blemishes, and infirmities.

But into this black night of man's awful sinning the promised Saviour is to come. He is to be the Star of Jacob, and a star is a glittering orb set in the canopy of universal darkness. It sparkles in the gloom. It sends forth its cheering light into the pall enveloping the earth. Such is Jesus our Lord. Oh, what loveliness there is in Him! He who is "over all, God blessed for ever" has become visible to the sons of men and has shone into our black night as "the brightness of His [the Father's] glory, and the express image of His Person" (Heb. 1:3). Light from heaven shines in the Star of Jacob. All that God is,

224

is made manifest in Him. What brightness shines when He appears! What loveliness is spread upon the soul when it perceives the Star of heavenly light!

THE SCEPTER OF ISRAEL

"A Scepter shall rise out of Israel." There is a mystic union between the Star and the Scepter. He, who first came to shine as light into our darkness and bring with Him a cheering ray of hope in a hopeless world, comes also to reign and rule in the hearts which He conquers. They lay down their arms of rebellion and acknowledge that He is Lord. In this generation, "the kingdom of God is within you"—that is, our Lord has a spiritual and beneficent rule in the hearts of His redeemed ones. There is no peace until He sits on the throne of the heart. There can be no love until He is loved as Saviour of our souls and the ruling King on the throne of our lives.

But more. He is the Scepter which shall smite this rebellious world until "the kingdoms of this world are become the kingdoms of our Lord, and of His Christ; and He shall reign for ever and ever" (Rev. 11:15). This is what is meant by the word: He "shall smite the corners of Moab, and destroy all the children of Sheth" (Num. 24:17). The wicked are to be overthrown by Him at His appearing. They are to lie down in sorrow. They are to be destroyed. Alas for those who have to say with Balaam: "I shall see Him, but not now: I shall behold Him, but not nigh." The wicked are to see Him come in power and glory. When He calls His ransomed ones, these are to stand afar off. How sad the words "but not nigh." When the Scepter rules over the Father's vast dominions, His elect bride, the company of the redeemed, will be at His side to share His governmental authority and rule. This is the completion of believers' prayers and joys. They shall have nothing more to ask for: no more, indeed, could they want. All hail, Thou Star of Jacob! Make haste, O Thou Scepter of Israel!

Hail, Thou once despised Jesus!
Hail, Thou still rejected King!

Thou didst suffer to release us;
Thou didst free salvation bring.
Through Thy death and resurrection,
Bearer of our sin and shame!
We enjoy divine protection,
Life and glory through Thy Name.

Jesus hail! enthroned in glory,
There forever to abide;
All the heavenly hosts adore Thee,
Seated at Thy Father's side:
There for sinners Thou art pleading,
There Thou dost our place prepare,
Ever for us interceding
Till in glory we appear.

Worship, honor, power, and blessing
Thou art worthy to receive;
Loudest praises, without ceasing,
Meet it is for us to give.
Help ye bright angelic spirits,
Bring your sweetest, noblest lays;
Help to sing our Saviour's merits,
Help to chant Immanuel's praise.

—JOHN BAKEWELL

52

The Blessed Hope in the Lord's Supper

...Till He come.

1 CORINTHIANS 11:26

There is a forward-looking hope in the Lord's Supper. Our Lord left His disciples on the Mount of Olivet over against Bethany. His many appearances during the forty days which He spent on earth after His resurrection had given them a new confidence, so that they returned to Jerusalem with joy and praise (Lk. 24:50-53). They were assured of His coming again. The Lord's Supper is a constant reminder of this return and is the pledge of it. "For as often as ye eat this bread, and drink this cup, ye do show the Lord's death till He come" (1 Cor. 11:26).

THE COMFORT IT IMPARTS

"Wherefore comfort one another with these words" (1 Thess. 4:18). This passage has to do with the Apostle Paul's assurance to believers concerning those who had already died in the Lord. What he wrote, he tells us very clearly, he received from the Lord. It came direct from heaven and by divine revelation from the Lord Himself.

Therefore, we are not to sorrow about those departed in the Lord.

227

The Lord's return is the day of final redemption, both for those who have departed and for those who still remain on the earth at that day. We may not know the day or the hour, but we do know that "the night is far spent" that is, the long dark night of man's rebellion. We also know that "the day is at hand" that is, the day of the Lord's glorious appearance for His own. He is coming to take us out of this murky house, this idolatrous Egypt, this worldly Babylon, and that assurance is to be a continual comfort to the saints.

THE VIGILANCE IT REQUIRES

There is always the peril of stagnation and of settling down. We are not to have a mere sentimental longing for the Lord's return. It is, after all, a day of solemn investigation, for we are to appear before His judgment seat, not to be called into account for our sins, which have already been judged at Calvary's cross, but to have our service evaluated and, if possible, rewarded. Let us not be among those who say, "Where is the promise of His coming?" or among those who say, "My Lord delayeth His coming." He will not stay away a moment longer than necessary for the accomplishment of His purpose. His word is "Watch! Be ready!"

This weekly gathering at the Lord's Supper should inspire us with spiritual vigilance. It should be our desire to go out to meet Him with open and glad countenance, and not with a sense of shame. Any Roman of ancient times, when confronted with some unworthy proposal, thought it sufficient refusal to say, *Romanus sum*—"I am a Roman!" Surely every form of temptation to sin should be met by believers declaring themselves to be the Lord's, as Joseph said to Potiphar's wife: "How...can I do this great wickedness, and sin against God?" (Gen. 39:9) Constant attendance at the Lord's Supper will help us to do this very thing and to watch our souls with all diligence.

THE GODLINESS IT INSPIRES

"Every man that hath this hope in him purifieth himself, even as He is pure" (1 Jn. 3:3). "What manner of persons ought ye to be in

228

all holy conversation and godliness, looking for and hasting unto the coming of the day of God" (2 Pet. 3:11-12). Each returning Lord's Day should find us a little further along the heavenward way, with our eye and heart and hope resting in heavenly and abiding things. "Our conversation [whole manner of life] is in heaven; from whence also we look for the Saviour, the Lord Jesus Christ" (Phil. 3:20).

Oh, that the Lord would revive our desire for inward holiness, our love for the brethren, and our devotion to the Lord Himself in view of His soon appearing! I doubt not that the right partaking of the Lord's Supper, with proper spiritual exercises of worship and adoration, praise and thanksgiving, will best inspire us to this godly walk. In the presence of holy things we are made to feel that everything which belongs to the earth sphere is more and more repulsive, and things heavenly and spiritual are more and more satisfying and sanctifying.

THE HOPE IT ENGENDERS

We are to behold His glory. "Father," our Lord prayed in John 17:24, "I will that they also, whom Thou hast given Me, be with Me where I am; that they may behold My glory." What a sight that will be! "If being a Christian were only to see the face of the royal Prince of heaven," said saintly Samuel Rutherford, "then it were a well-spent journey, though we have to creep through seven deaths and seven hells of suffering to behold Him." The curtains which veil His glory now are to be rolled back, and we are to see Him as He is. In that day we shall have resurrection bodies which will be capable (which our present bodies are not) of beholding that glory.

Not only are we to behold that glory, but we ourselves are to obtain glory. "He called you by our gospel, to the obtaining of the glory of our Lord Jesus Christ" (2 Thess. 2:14). Like a bridegroom on his wedding day, our Lord will appear all glorious. But shall His beloved bride appear in rags on the occasion of her being united to Him? Surely not! She, too, must be radiant with glory; indeed she shall be the wonder of the universe!

The Lord has gone to prepare a home for us in the heavens. There

229

we shall be at home with Him whom we love, and also with our true kindred—those who love Him, too. It will be a paradise of happiness forever, a place into which no foe shall ever come, and out of which no friend shall ever depart. There the glorious Lord, in the midst of the throne, shall lead His people to living fountains of water, and God shall wipe away all tears from their eyes.

> *"Till He come!"*
> *O let the words*
> *Linger on the trembling chords;*
> *Let the "little while" between*
> *In their golden light be seen;*
> *Let us think how heaven and home*
> *Lie beyond that "Till He come!"*
>
> *When the weary ones we love*
> *Enter on their rest above,*
> *When their words of love and cheer*
> *Fall no longer on our ear,*
> *Hush! be every murmur dumb,*
> *It is only "Till He come!"*
>
> *Clouds and darkness round us press;*
> *Would we have one sorrow less?*
> *All the sharpness of the cross,*
> *All that tells the world is loss,*
> *Death, and darkness, and the tomb*
> *Pain us only "Till He come"*
>
> *Sweet the feast of love divine,*
> *Broken bread and outpoured wine;*
> *Sweet memorials, till the Lord*
> *Call us round His heav'nly board,*
> *Some from earth, from glory some,*
> *Severed only "Till He come!"*

—EDWARD H. BICKERSTETH

53

An Autobiographical Sketch

Daniel Smith lived a life remarkable for its almost endless variety. Born in England of Scottish stock, he carried the gospel to the farthest reaches of China, Burma, India, and Ceylon (now Sri Lanka). He preached extensively in England, Australia, New Zealand, Canada, and the United States. He knew Gypsy Smith and Samuel Chadwick, Bakht Singh and Watchman Nee. He co-labored with Joe Blinko (who later served with the Billy Graham Association), and with D. E. Hoste, one of the famous Cambridge Seven, and Director of the China Inland Mission. He boldly took opportunities to share God's Word with Queen Elizabeth, Mamie Eisenhower, and a multitude of others. Hundreds came to Christ through his ministry. These excerpts are from his autobiography, Pilgrim of the Heavenly Way.

MY BIRTH AND LINEAGE

I was born on the first day of April, 1907, which is referred to as April Fools' Day. It was so before I was born! The place of my birth was Thornaby-on-Tees, Yorkshire, England. The town at one time was known as South Stockton but in my day had its own municipality. Stockton proper is on the Durham side of the River Tees; Thornaby on the Yorkshire side. I was the second child of my parents, John and Janet Brash Smith. My people were Scottish and their nationalism was an entrenched pride. Before me was Helen, and five followed me—James, John, Grace, Christina, and Janet.

Father was descended from a rather rough line, though he himself was not really so, having been influenced by my mother and molded to some extent by Presbyterianism. He believed in God and in the essential truths of the Christian faith, and at one time was on the Manager's Board of the church. But his father, my grandfather, Daniel by name, was a seagoing engineer who boasted some pirating ventures. He was an adventurer of sorts and used to tell stories of pirating ships in foreign coastal waters. The things of God were far from his mind.

It was said that our name Smith was *Gow* in Gaelic and it was supposed that we Smiths were descended from the infamous Scottish John Gow or Smith who commanded "The Revenge" and was hung by the neck in London in the year 1725 for piracy. It has been difficult to ascertain the truth of this, and I have not researched the roots of my lineage. But in the days when seagoing men were poorly paid, grandfather always came home with plenty of money. Each time he made landfall, he would take me off to be rigged out in a sailor's suit or a Scottish kilt and then have me photographed with him. I was a favorite boy of his.

Mother came from a more godly line. Her maiden name was Brash and her background was Scottish Covenanter stock. The history of the Covenanters was a glorious but bloody page in Scottish history. They rose in the seventeenth century in opposition to the Papacy which became strong and oppressive under the reign of Mary, Queen of Scots. Presbyterian leaders were scandalized when Mary allowed the Roman mass to be celebrated in Holyrood palace. The country was then plunged into violent turmoil and godly men arose to defend what they called "the crown rights of the Redeemer."

Later, after Mary had been executed by her cousin, Elizabeth, Queen of England, James VI of Scotland became James I of England. To placate the English, he became an ardent advocate of the Church of England ritual and control of the Church by the prelacy. One of the king's decrees was that all church members receive the communion elements at the hands of a bishop while kneeling before him, a form of superstition and idolatry. It was from events such as these that Scottish people inherited a detestation of prelacy, the leaven of man's invention, and against the testimony of God's holy Word. I, too, imbibed something of this, and some measure of that extreme Calvinism which prevailed in Scotland.

A SOUND CONVERSION

There were deep impressions wrought through the Presbyterian ministry which made me look seriously into my heart. Ministers were scholarly and evangelical, and one series on great missionaries was particularly affecting. It seemed so wonderful that the Lord had chosen such people, led them to the right countries, endowed them with gifts and courage, and that they accomplished so much good. I marvelled that their sympathies could reach out so far, and that love could so motivate them as to leave their own culture, customs, and comforts, to spend their lives teaching ignorant savages, and ofttimes to lay down their lives in sacrifice. The three which affected me most were John Paton of the New Hebrides, Mary Slessor of Calabar, and William Carey of India.

One Sunday a Dr. Elmslie preached from Revelation 3:20, "Behold, I stand at the door and knock…" He was a learned scholar and notable singer. In the course of his message, he broke into song,

Behold Me standing at the door,
And hear Me pleading evermore,
Say, weary heart, oppressed with sin,
May I come in? May I come in?

I was overwhelmed and melted, but how to open my heart's door I did not know. It seemed stuck.

But help was at hand. My father's most respected apprentice was Joe Wilkin—a fine, born again lad. He was a Methodist and invited me to what he called "a class meeting." The leader, Wilfrid Fountain, was an insurance agent, and he examined each of the class as to their spiritual state. I had never heard such testimonies or descriptions of

233

state in the Presbyterian Church. These all knew the Lord and I felt like a speckled bird among them. But Wilfrid made God's way and method very clear. As we knelt in prayer, without being asked for any decision, there was a revelation of the Lord Jesus in me. I suddenly knew Him to be the Lamb of God who had purchased my redemption with the sacrifice of Himself. He was the Bridge I had been seeking and I was enabled to commit myself into His hands to be saved by Him. The words He said to Thomas came alive to me: "Reach hither," and I put my hands that night into the pierced hands of the One who "loved me and gave Himself for me." He was to me, as to Thomas, "My Lord and my God," and I was heartily willing at that moment to be His.

Toward the end of my eighteenth year, I felt my whole life should be devoted to the Lord and to His service. Life was no longer negative and meaningless, but now seemed to be something that was to be framed by the hand of my Saviour's love.

A SPECIFIC CALL

The years since conversion were now seen by me as a tremendous lesson in God's guidance. There was impelling power driving me on. There was also repelling power restraining and holding back until there was a measure of spiritual fitness.

The verse which the Lord had given me earlier, "Ask of Me, and I shall give thee the heathen for thine inheritance, and the uttermost parts of the earth for thy possession" (Ps. 2:8), now resurrected within me with new life and meaning. Evangelism at home began to lose its magic grip and, in its place, came a burden for those in "the uttermost parts of the earth."

About this time a friend sent me a biography of Hudson Taylor by Marshall Broomhall—*The Man Who Believed God.* The principles and practices of the mission which he founded—the China Inland Mission—greatly appealed to me, especially that of living in total dependence on the Lord for the supply of all daily needs. It seemed that, as I read, a gentle hand was beckoning me both to China and to the China Inland Mission.

234

Then again, Miss Mildred Cable, author of *Ambassadors for Christ,* and who, with Francesca and Evangeline French, pioneered the Gobi Desert in China under the auspices of the Mission, came to the college to tell of their journeys. She was a woman of spiritual discernment and we all sat spellbound at the courage and daring of these three intrepid and brave women of God. I asked a question from the floor and after the meeting closed, Mildred Cable came down the aisle, stood, looked me in the eye, and said, "Young man, I believe the Lord would have you consider China."

SHANGHAI HEADQUARTERS

In 1934, after preparation and training, I arrived in China—a land which had always been a land of mystery to me. Its people have a history stretching back to 4000 BC, though beyond the reign of Fu Hsi, 2852 BC, that history is shrouded in the mystical and legendary. Fu Hsi is said to have taught his people to fish with nets, to play the lute and lyre, to have insisted on strict laws governing marriage, and to have invented the hieroglyphic system of writing. The Chinese are a remarkable people—industrious and philosophical, and, until recent times, have hardly been influenced by the rest of the world.

The General Director of the Mission was Mr. D. E. Hoste. He was one of the famous "Cambridge Seven"—seven Cambridge university graduates who were called to China. One other of the seven, the best known, was C. T. Studd, the English cricketer.

Mr. Hoste was a man of dignity and discernment. Quiet in his ways, he was a man of real spiritual stature. He had followed Hudson Taylor as General Director of the Mission, a position he held for about the same length of time as Mr. Hudson Taylor—35 years. He had his spiritual upbringing among the people with whom I fellowship, and whom he jokingly referred to as "the PB's."

My first contact with Mr. Hoste brought blushes to my face. Racing upstairs in the Shanghai headquarters, I had charged into him. He smiled as though nothing had happened and asked my name.

"Smith, sir, Daniel Smith, sir."

"Praise the Lord," said he, "It was a bad day for Israel when there were no smiths in it." This was a reference to 1 Samuel 13:19, "Now there was no smith found throughout all the land of Israel, for the Philistines said, Lest the Hebrews make them swords and spears." By taking the smiths captive, the Philistines made Israel weak in warfare through lack of weaponry.

"Would you like to walk with me one day?" he enquired. What could I say? He was the man of authority in the Mission and I but a new recruit. Yet he was asking as though it would be a favor to him. His greatness, like that of Moses, was in his meekness. He was never immoderate in his words nor harsh in his censures.

Shanghai was a place full of beggars. One day we went walking round the block and were accosted by as many as fifteen beggars. To each of them Mr. Hoste gave a little alms. His hand was always open to relieve the poor and he spared them what he could from his little store. No one was refused.

"Did you notice anything while we were walking, dear brother?" he asked on our return.

I replied that I noticed he had given something to every beggar who asked of him.

"Yes, brother," said he with a loving arm around my shoulder, "never shut up the bowels of compassion against the poor." He felt the wants and sorrows of those in need, and would relieve their necessities as he had opportunity. Those were days when indigenous principles (making sure nationals did not become dependent on foreign workers) were being insisted upon, and rightly so. But some missionaries were pushing principles to such an extent as to dry up all human compassion. How blessed it is to have a pitying eye, sentiments of compassion and generosity, and a heart which overflows in unrestrained benevolence. All such had Mr. Hoste.

Another day he invited me to pray with him. Naturally enough, I thought we would pray in turn, so I went with a storehouse of matters for prayer. One of the first things which affected me was the atmosphere of his presence. I understood what James meant when he spoke of the prayers of "a righteous man" availing much (Jas. 5:16). Here was not only prayer, but the prayers of a holy and mature man

236

of God, prayers which no doubt had the ear and attention of the Lord. Mr. Hoste prayed—and prayed for four-and-a-half hours! Remember, these were his *private* prayers, and I was being allowed into his closet. Sometimes he would kneel, then stand, then walk, while he prayed. There were eight hundred missionaries in the Mission. He knew them all by name without looking at a book—and all their needs, and their three hundred children! As for me, my knees were riveted to the floor. I couldn't move. I was filled with awe and reverential fear. In this secret place of prayer, Mr. Hoste was at home with God. It was his chief pleasure.

Finally he touched me on the shoulder. "Dear brother," he said as I rose, "I thought you might be hungry." Then rather wistfully: "You know, we've only prayed for China."

He would yet pray more. He prayed for many in scores of countries—for men of every race and for all classes of people. The whole world was on his heart. And this prayer session was no special thing. It was his daily exercise and I was only in on part of it, albeit a four-and-a-half-hour part. What a lesson! What a way of teaching!

The Door of Hope Mission in Shanghai was a remarkable rescue work for girls exposed, and sometimes committed, to lives of shame, vice, and misery. Miss Gladys Dieterie superintended the work and, inviting me to speak to the girls, took me aside afterwards like a mother in Israel to instill a lesson which I would never forget.

Her simple prescription for all difficult situations was "putting the Lord in the midst." It was a reference to the time when our Lord took three disciples with Him up into "the Mount of Transfiguration." In the meantime, an anxious father had brought his demon-possessed boy to those other disciples who had not gone up the mount. These had no answer to the problem and could give no relief to his dilemma (Mt. 17:14-16).

Those who went with the Lord were "eye-witnesses of His majesty" as He was transfigured before them. They saw His sovereignty and knew His power. These three then escorted the Lord down the mount and brought Him into the midst of that situation in the valley. The power of Satan was then broken and the unhappy boy delivered from the devil's grip.

"Do you see, brother," said this mature woman of God, "you are going into the interior where all is in Satan's hands and where demonic forces tend to arrest and smother the Lord's testimony. The merely nominal can never break through. You have to ascend into spiritual elevation and see the Lord in His majesty, that He is the Lord—the Sovereign Lord. Then by faith, place Him in the midst of every situation." What lessons for a young missionary!

MY ENGAGEMENT

The prospects of marriage were dim for me in eastern Yunnan where I was serving. There was no young missionary lady in the high mountain vastnesses among the aborigines. I was a bachelor missionary and marriage was as distant from my mind as girls were from my present circumstance.

Travelling some days' journey from my home in Salowu, I came on the return to Wuting, to the home of the Simpkins. It was customary among many of the missionaries to pray for the workers in each province after the morning or evening meal, after reading their names from the Mission directory. The Simpkins had just finished their evening meal and were reading the names of those in our own province when I slipped in the door to surprise them. As I did so, I heard a name being read by Theo: Catherine McGlashan.

In Christian experience there are times when the Spirit of God makes a verse or promise of Scripture alive and applicable. It has your name on it, so to speak. It is directed to you in a personal way. Something of the same was now my case. That name charmed me. Whoever Catherine McGlashan was, I knew she was for me! There was a kind of inner registration from the Spirit of God and the verse, at the top of the page for the day was: "I will give them one heart, and one way" (Jer. 32:39).

Cathie was in the west of the province, working among the Chinese near where the Frasers, Kuhns, and others labored on the higher slopes among the Lisu of the Salween valley. I was in the east of the same province, among the Nosu. Before the Burma road was

238

built, 27 days' journey by horse travel separated Kunming, the capital city lying in the east of the province from Erhyuan in the west, where Cathie had her home among the Chinese.

I knew nothing of this Catherine McGlashan. Whether she was fat or slim, tall or short, pretty or homely, clever or otherwise; I had no idea! But I did have this inner registration of the Spirit of God that she was to be my wife. I asked no question and made no inquiries.

Twelve months went by. The matter almost faded from my memory after so long a time. After all, there was no contact, nor had I ever seen anything written of her or by her. The Lord Himself would have to bring us together. Then suddenly He stirred me up to the remembrance of her. One day a young missionary fellow came from the west. The need for dental work had brought him to the capital city of Kunming. Hearing of God's great movement among the Nosu, he decided to come the additional six days' journey north to see me. We had been in language school together and so were good friends. As any young man will, he talked one night about his hopes of marriage. There were three young women out west, and it was his declared intention to propose to one of them on return. There were three young men in that area, and reason might well have concluded that they would come together in pairs.

"And whom have you chosen, brother?" I asked.

"Catherine McGlashan!" said he.

Once again there was that name and once again it came in that living way with the assurance that Catherine was to be my wife. Even in the face of this challenge, I felt perfect peace in my heart. No questions were asked, and I still knew nothing more about her when my friend left than I had known before. She was still a mystery.

Twelve more months passed, and again the thought of her seemed to fade away. It was the time of the Nosu awakening. There were many meetings, calls, and demands, and life was tremendously thrilling but exhausting. Missionary friends in other places reported to headquarters in Shanghai that I was in need of a vacation. In due time, a letter arrived from the General Director, ordering a three-month rest at Chefoo on the northeast coastal province of Shantung, where the C. I. M. schools were located.

This meant a six-day journey south by horse to Kunming. From there, in those days, there was a train down through Vietnam to the port of Haiphong. A coastal steamer plied between Haiphong and Hong Kong, where I could transship and sail to the northern port of Chefoo. But when I arrived at Kunming, a telegram was waiting from the General Director. The port of Chefoo was in the grip of a great ice freeze and closed to shipping. The journey there would have to be postponed.

By this time the Burma road was partly built, and it was possible to travel by bus from Kunming to the only city of a few thousand residents in the far west—Tali. A further telegram arrived suggesting that I do this very thing—go to Tali. I went, and in going, greatly suspected the gentle hand of the Lord leading me to Cathie.

Cathie and Stella Kirkman were in Erhyuan, two days north of Tali. But it so happened in the Lord's providential arrangements that Mr. J. O. Fraser, the superintendent of West Yunnan, had scheduled a workers' conference in Tali the very day I was to arrive. Had it been any other time, or had there been no conference at all, I would not have met my Catherine. But the Lord's ways are perfect, and so it came about that, when I arrived, all the missionaries were in Tali—and Cathie, too! On the third day, she was walking alone in the garden. I joined her and told her all the story of two years of inward conviction. I had her attention.

We were engaged on the third day after meeting. Perhaps Scottish caution demanded three days—or was it, in Scriptural typology, resurrection day! Both of us were conscious that the Lord had led us to belong to each other. We might have been married without delay, but Mr. Fraser communicated the news to Shanghai and another telegram arrived advising me to take the vacation assigned before entering into the marriage state. We agreed. Now forty years have passed and I can say, "This thing proceeded from the Lord" (Gen. 24:50).

LIFE AMONG THE NOSU TRIBE

In the area north of Kunming, in the eastern part of Yunnan, there

240

are six tribes of Miao, Laga, Tai, Gopu, Lisu and Nosu. The Miao tribes are quite distinct—short and stocky. It would be hard to find another race which they resemble. There may be forty different tribes of them. The Lisu, Laga, Gopu and Nosu are inter-related somewhat, together with most of the Mantze (savage) tribes across the river Yangtze in the western part of Szechwan province.

The homes of the Nosu are more substantial than those of other tribes. The poorer tribes have houses made of hemp-sticks for walls and long grass for roofs. The better class Nosu would have roofs of tiles which they themselves fire in kilns, and boards with straw on trestles for beds rather than the earthen floor. Even so, they are poor dwelling places and afford no comfort to pamper Western flesh.

Our own home was a mud-brick structure. Water was brought from a spring about a quarter mile away by means of a flume of hollowed-out pine trees, then stored in a tower. We bought wheat from those who lived at lower altitudes, as, in these higher ones, nothing but bitter buckwheat was a safe crop. The wheat was periodically spread in the sun to rid it of weevils and was ground in a hand operated millstone, worked by the village girls. The cooking stove in the kitchen was mudbrick, and a built-in kerosene tin with a soldered lid served as an oven for bread making. Charcoal was our heating fuel, but care had to be taken when using it for warmth in a room. Carbon monoxide fumes could easily overcome and asphyxiate. Two horses were kept for travel, and two cows for a tardily given drop of milk. It was life in simplicity and very near to nature.

The tribes were animists all. To them, the trees, rocks, and the earth were full of immaterial intelligences which worked unceasingly to destroy them. With such beliefs, the moral state was low and the only pleasure known was sexual indulgence.

The languages of the tribes were monosyllabic and tonal. Compared to Chinese, which is classical and rich in expression, the tribal languages had severe limitations of words by reason of their seclusion from the rest of mankind. As they had no form of writing, missionaries had to invent one for them, and translation work was not at all easy. But in our area many young men went down to Chinese city schools, and this gave us some educated men who could read well, comprehending the Christian Chinese literature.

There were recompenses to the poor existence on those infertile mountaintops. It is no small gain for such peoples to have escaped the cares, burdens, and heart-hardening influences of the Western world. That freedom has kept their hearts kind and wonderfully hospitable. The deep deviltry of their religious beliefs is not the hardest core in human nature. They may well thank God that "the deceitfulness of riches" never came near them. It is, of course, neither riches nor penury but grace which saves. Nevertheless, we saw that, among the tribes, our blessed Lord had ready access to their lowly huts and many thousands of these peoples came to rest on the Saviour's breast. They had what many of the rich of this world and what many cultivated minds in every field of science never possessed. They gained the key to heaven while many proud philosophers grope without.

THE COMMUNIST CONQUEST

Modern China's revolutionary process goes back to 1911. Sun Yat Sen was the prophet of it and the revolution of that year brought to an end the rule of the Manchu dynasty which had ruled China from 1644. The Opium War of 1842 had opened certain ports to Britain, and Western powers took advantage of the increasing decay of the nation to gain leases from the Chinese of parcels of their territory. Sun Yat Sen resisted this growing takeover and espoused his philosophy in the *San Min Chu E—The Three Principles*. His three principles were nationalism, democracy, and the people's livelihood. Out from this arose the Kuomintang Party, and in 1927 Chiang Kai Shek established his authority as leader of it.

In 1934, Mao Tze Tung emerged in opposition to the Nationalist Party and organized the Communist Party. In that year he began the long march of six thousand miles which started with 90,000 men and ended with 20,000. They captured three of our missionaries on the way and the last one released, almost at the point of death was Mr. Bosshardt. They threw him out just outside Kunming and missionaries rescued him, nursing him back to life. His book, *The Restraining*

242

Hand, tells the gripping story of his amazing preservation.

While Generalissimo Chiang Kai Shek and his Nationalists fought the Japanese who had invaded the country, Mao strengthened his forces in seclusion in the north until they were a million strong. At the conclusion of the Japanese War, Mao picked his time to move. His forces were well disciplined and magnificently led by dedicated and efficient commanders. The Nationalists were weak and weary after years of struggle with the Japanese, so that the whole country was soon swallowed up by the Communists and named "The Republic of China" in 1949.

Our China Inland Mission thought it would be possible to work under any form of Chinese government, since the Chinese had always been so docile and conciliatory. We soon discovered, however, that the Chinese brand of Communism was far more extreme and virulent than the Russian type, so that difficult days lay ahead.

I may say here that Communism is the first great anti-God force to move on the face of the earth. In ancient times, mighty and cruel empires rose, such as the Persians, Greeks, and Romans. Perhaps no nation ever perpetrated such cruelties as the Assyrian hordes. But all these ancient empires were, in a sense, religious. They were idolatrous and superstitious, yet religious in a way. The atrocities of the Assyrians, for instance, all were done in the name of their god—Asshut. Communism is something else. It is a profane, atheistic, materialistic, godless movement which is both anti-false god and anti-true God—a brutal engine for the destruction of men's souls and the enslavement of their bodies.

Leaving our Beloved China

Eventually it became impossible to stay. We were instructed to leave along the Burma Road—the only missionaries whom they allowed to leave by the backdoor. All others had to go the long route east across the country and exit either by Shanghai or Canton.

We were afterwards to see the purpose of the Lord in this. A new and fruitful ministry for us was to spring up in Ceylon (now Sri Lanka), India, and Pakistan, where I would be led into new associations which were to greatly enlarge and enrich my spiritual life.

Burma is surrounded on three sides by mountains and by the sea on its south. Maybe because of its being fenced in, it has always been very insular and has preserved its own distinctive culture. Beauty and dignity walk hand in hand there. I think it was Anawrahta who first fashioned its diverse peoples into a single kingdom and founded the first Burmeal Empire in the eleventh century. He himself had become a convert to Theravada Buddhism and almost overnight made his empire a Buddhist stronghold.

In the course of history, three wars with Britain finally annexed Burma in 1890 to the British Empire, but in its present state of independence, Burma is deeply troubled with insurgent uprisings in remote areas difficult to control.

The country was thick jungle where we entered from China, and since it was late afternoon when we crossed the border, it was not long before darkness began to fall, and the shrieking, roarings, and yelpings of wild beasts could be heard. How Satan delights to torment! If it isn't one thing, it's another! But then, we, the Lord's people, are His peculiar treasure. "He careth for you," says 1 Peter 5:7, and, sure enough, we suddenly had another manifestation of this when we came upon a bamboo cottage and found the folk in it were believers. In the heart of the jungle it seemed beyond belief! But we were soon made welcome. After a good night of sleep and refreshing hospitality, we were sent on our way to Lashio.

The bridge over the Irrawaddy at Mandalay had been destroyed in the war. It was necessary, therefore, to take a plane to Rangoon. Our family stayed over the weekend so that I could minister in the Burmese Christian church. A kind Norwegian captain of a freighter housed us in his hospital berth on board ship and thus it was that we came to Colombo, the capital city of Ceylon.

Now known as Sri Lanka, Ceylon lies off the southern tip of India like a teardrop. It has a continuous record of civilized life for more than 2,000 years. The Portuguese began the western penetration of the island, followed by the Dutch, who ruled it from 1658 to 1796. Then Britain took over, and so Ceylon was annexed to the Empire.

Sri Lanka is a most beautiful island, less than 300 miles in length and densely populated, with eight million Sinhalese and three million Tamils (at time of writing). The former are the dominant race and troubles have arisen through the imposition of Sinhalese as the official language.

The people are somewhat gentle when no racial strife inflames passion. It is almost a universal habit with them to chew betel nut and to spit copious streams of red saliva anywhere and everywhere. Their festivals are full of pomp and pageantry, and have religious significance. Colored and richly decorated elephants are always prominent. These are the chief haulers of industry, too, and well able to lift a thousand pounds' weight with their trunks.

Firewalking is one of the spectaculars on such festive occasions. I recall a rather foolish young Methodist minister who, soon after arrival, began, with a show of arrogance, to ridicule this particular feat. It came to public controversy and was climaxed by the young minister accepting a challenge to walk the white-hot cinders. Needless to say, Tenderfoot landed in the hospital with burnt and blistered feet. He knew too little about devildom.

A Word to Queen Elizabeth

Sri Lanka has always been one of the strongholds of Buddhism. It was made so by Mahinda, the son of an Indian king, Asoka, who is sometimes spoken of as the Constantine of Buddhism. In 246 BC, Mahinda accomplished the conversion of Ceylon in 26 days of preaching by winning the then ruler of Ceylon, together with a multitude of the principal people, to the doctrines of Buddha. Thereafter, a long line of kings of Ceylon were devoted Buddhists and from this island Buddhism spread to all countries east of the Ganges, including Burma, Thailand, and Vietnam. Sri Lanka remains to this day one of the strongholds of that system.

Buddhism is not a religion, strictly speaking. It is a philosophy of man's own invention which has issued in peculiar characteristics among the masses of the East—such as an easy indifference to life, a carelessness to duty, a general depression in seeking annihilation as

245

the goal of life, a selfishness which can be mean and violent, and a skepticism which leaves nothing worthy of effort. It degrades its adherents because there is no power to transform the inner life. It is a futile system of man's own effort to lift himself out of the mire.

When the present Queen of England was Princess Elizabeth, she began a tour which was to take her to Africa, Ceylon, Australia, and New Zealand. Britain was very anxious that Ceylon, having gained her independence, should adhere to the Commonwealth. The visit of the Princess was to help woo them to that adherence. Those making arrangements for the royal visit evidently knew very little of the intricacies of Buddhism. It is, as I have said, not strictly a religion, but modern disciples have tried to make it so, even referring to Buddha as Lord Buddha.

The man Buddha lived about 500 BC and was a Hindu prince who, in his search for the meaning of life, left his wife and infant son, and came into some kind of supposed enlightenment while sitting under a bo tree. His name was Siddhartha Gautama, but after this experience, he was called "The Buddha" or "The Enlightened One."

Buddha made no claim to divine origin, nor did he recognize the living God. He did not accept the account of creation nor believe in heaven. He fashioned a code of conduct and nothing more. The strongest emphasis in his system of thought was transmigration—the supposed return of the soul to other forms of life on earth. Bad men could come back as snakes; good men as princes. There is nothing which has the faintest relation to, or sanction from, the Word of God. He simply taught a life of self-imposed discipline to keep the soul between the two extremes: self-indulgence and self-mortification.

His wisdom was not the wisdom which is of God. There is no story of redemption. There is nothing of that blessed One who came down from heaven, assumed our human nature, and laid down His life for the sheep by offering Himself a sacrifice for the sins of all His people. Buddhists know nothing of the love He has declared, and continually shows for them by appearing in the presence of God on their behalf. Whatever enlightenment Buddha had, it was not spiritual enlightenment, and he remained ignorant of the blessings of grace

246

which spring from the matchless love of Christ.

To placate the new independent government of Ceylon, it was arranged that the Princess would go to the most venerated of all temples where the supposed tooth of Buddha, the most prized of all relics, lay in a casket. In that temple she was to remove her shoes, enter into the inner sanctum, and cast an offering of gold at the feet of Buddha's image. This, in the Buddhist mind, is identification, and would make the Princess a Buddhist. The newspapers made much of this, and Buddhists were full of glee.

But there came a remarkable intervention. When the Princess and her husband, Philip, Duke of Edinburgh, whom she had married on November 20, 1947, were in Kenya, her father, King George VI, died. The Princess had to return to London to attend the funeral, take the oath of accession, and prepare for her coronation service, which took place on June 2, 1953.

It was during this period that I wrote a letter to the Queen. In this I pointed out that the arrangements for her tour, which she promised to resume, had enmeshed her in Buddhism, and that these arrangements amounted to an identification with that system. I dared to remind Her Majesty that this would wound the hearts of the Lord's people in Ceylon, mar her own title as Defender of the Faith, darken the glory of the gospel in this strongly Buddhist country, and weaken the hands and maybe imperil the lives of national believers.

The matter was brought to the Queen's personal attention, and her private secretary wrote me that Her Majesty had commanded cancellation of any visit to any temple. She kept her word.

"By me kings reign," says the Word of God in Proverbs 8:15, and therefore there was the purpose of God wrapped up in Princess Elizabeth becoming queen. I have mentioned one providential intervention and counter-working to preserve that purpose. The government of this world is upon the shoulders of the Lord Jesus Christ and, having all power in heaven and earth, guards and preserves His own interests, manifestly doing so on this occasion in the life of Queen Elizabeth.

Our sovereign kings and queens need to guard against the snares of Satan, for what they do affects many people. Their undertakings need the approval and blessing of the Lord, and this includes all civil as well as sacred duties. Politicians may spin their subtle contrivances, but happy is the king or queen who is in touch with the throne of God.

THE CONQUEROR OF MOUNT EVEREST

It was on one of our tours of evangelism to the north that I met Tensing Norkay, the conqueror—together with Edmund Hillary of New Zealand—of the highest mountain on the earth's surface. Everything in the region of Sikkim Tibet, Nepal, and Bhutan is gigantic. We were having evangelistic campaigns at this time in Darjeeling and Kalimpong. Tibetans were very numerous in our Town Hall meetings and we found them to be a kindly, humorous, but often drunken people.

Darjeeling lies at the foot of the Kanchenjunga, third highest mountain range, towering 28,146 feet into the sky. When darkness falls on the town, the rays of the hidden sun still linger for some time on the top of the Kanchenjunga. The head of the range is very much like a crown and, at evening time, it stands out like gold in the heavens. It is a magnificent spectacle.

Several Nepalese believers were to be baptized here, and for that we decided on a river about two miles out of town. The walk there would provide opportunity for witness so all believers went in procession—singing as we went. As we marched, we passed the home of Tensing, which the Indian government had bought for him following his successful climb. He was a Sherpa tribesman, and the Sherpas on the Indian side were very much like our Nosu friends on the China side of the heights. As we sang and passed his home, he came out to watch and listen.

Back in Yunnan, China, our British Consul was Sir Eric Shipton, one of England's most famous mountaineers. He had led many of the expeditions in attempts to conquer Everest. Indeed it was he who discovered the way by which it was finally conquered. The Shiptons lived just a little way from the Mission Home in Kunming. When the

Communists took over, they snubbed the British recognition of their regime and consuls were ignored. In those days neither he nor we could do very much, and at times the Shiptons would entertain, he often telling stories of his exploits.

On our way back from the baptisms at Darjeeling, Tensing and his family came out once more to see and hear our procession of witness. His home was well guarded with twenty-five Tibetan dogs. In a land of thievery he needed them. Gifts of great value had been sent to him from many notable personages in many countries. However, no one who respected his life would venture near his place. His Tibetan dogs looked and sounded as fierce as evening wolves.

There was a gardener working near the gate as we passed by. Remembering that Eric Shipton was Tensing's old leader, I sent the Sherpa a booklet by the hand of the gardener with a note to say that I was a friend of the Shiptons. In a few minutes the man came running for me. Tensing wanted to see me. Would I please come?

Tensing was very amiable and pleasant. He had a broad smile which displayed a magnificent set of teeth. The simple Sherpa is wise and thoughtful, though he has known little of formal education. As leader of the porters on many expeditions, he had also companied with notable men, gleaned a good deal of wisdom, and could speak five languages. He gave me a warm Sherpa greeting and wanted to know all about his old friend and leader.

He asked whether I would like to look over his many gifts. But I suggested that we sit while I talked to him about a mountain that he had never climbed. So for almost two hours, I told Tensing the meaning of the cross of Christ. A Christian on the team that conquered Everest had spoken to him several times so that he had heard something of the gospel. He had heard it, too, from Sherpa believers in Darjeeling. I now had time to make the salvation story crystal clear. I told how the Lord loved us, even when we were unlovely; and died for us while we were yet sinners. I set before him the mysteries of His grace, and how we could be saved and justified from all our sins. And I saw there was such attention to God's Word that I believed the Holy Spirit was drawing his heart out after the Lord.

"Shall we pray, Tensing? Would you like me to pray?" Tensing went to the foot of the stairs and called all his family to come for prayer. I believe Tensing became the Lord's. I trust I shall see him in heaven's glory, that Tensing Norkay will be part of the Saviour's spoil from the Sherpas of the high Himalayas.

GOD'S WORK IN GOD'S WAY

In my now advancing years, I have come to believe that a local church is the nearest expression on earth to the truth of our Lord's universal church. Looking back over my life with one of the most respected faith missions, the weakness of such missions became apparent on our evacuation from China. Missionaries of such missions are not sent out directly by local churches, and therefore had no local churches to which they could return to find care and sustenance until rehabilitated. Many who served our mission for thirty or forty years were suddenly laid off from the active fellowship, and that in the matter of a month or so. Some who went out in their early twenties did not have a profession or trade which they could take up again. This brought them into very trying circumstances. It would appear to me now that such missions are lacking a vital element in God's order. Outgoing missionaries are not loved, cared for, provided for, as when sent out and commended by a local church in the biblical manner.

Also there is an obedience to human directorship which severely limits one's personal leading by the Spirit of God. Missionaries have sometimes been sent to places simply because there were mission buildings to occupy. In being sent by a local assembly, with freedom to move as the Spirit leads, I believe there is behind such missionaries an intimate prayer support and a godly care that cements us all the more to the one center, Christ the Lord. I think such missionaries move with free and glad hearts. Under the love and care and protection of a home assembly, they can set forth, submissive to the guidance of the Holy Spirit. They can be well assured that He will not set them in the wrong place, nor lead them in the wrong path, nor endow them with wrong or manufactured gifts.

It is much the same with Bible schools. Good as they may be, they do not reach up to God's plan in Holy Scripture. A properly functioning assembly is the best and most natural place for instruction in heavenly things and the best training ground for service. In such a group, all are in one local body and all made to drink of one Spirit (1 Cor. 12:12-13), and are made utterly dependent on the Spirit of God for spiritual exercise. It is the assembly which is the special sphere of the Holy Spirit's activity, where He best enriches and bestows His gifts.

Such spiritual principles laid down in Scripture are designed to bring believers into a certain divine order which can make even "unlearned and ignorant men" mighty in the Scriptures. Bible schools are a human scheme to develop spiritual gift and an honest attempt to compensate for the low measure of spirituality in the churches. But there are perils in being trained there rather than in local assemblies. One of the perils is to assume spiritual gifts which may not have been given by the Spirit of God nor wrought out by personal spiritual exercise. God's own plan is the most advantageous. The life of the believer must be demonstrated amidst a communal life in a holy walk, and in the local assembly gift is tested and proved. I often wish that I had known the pattern of heavenly things in earlier days. I am sure I would not be so scant in ministerial ability, and maybe my little candle might have shed a warmer and brighter light through these many years.

You will have noticed that I was brought up in the Presbyterian church, saved in the Methodist, ordained in the Baptist, spent many years with the interdenominational China Inland Mission, and also labored three years with a Bible Institute. None of these changes were brought about by a discontented spirit of fault-finding with this or that; but all were a progressive leading onwards by the Spirit of God. Spiritual history for me has been a spiritual journey. It was nothing in the primary sense—neither technical nor doctrinal—which passed me on from one to another, out of this into that, but just a kind of spiritual ongoing led by the Spirit of God. Eventually I was led into association with New Testament assemblies where I have

251

found that which most closely resembles what I see to be God's design in His Word. Perhaps I could sum up what this fellowship has meant to me in four ways.

First, a new freedom. In my spiritual pilgrimage, the Lord has taken much away from me—my evangelistic work on the staff of Cliff College, my service in China, Baptist churches where I served, my ministry in Ceylon, my association with Bakht Singh in India, my connection with Prairie Bible Institute in Canada. Besides these parts of service, there has been the loss of possessions, a library of books in China, and constant separations from wife and children.

These losses, however, have never been viewed by me as negative things. The Lord has always been so real and precious before my eyes that I have been enabled to take everything as from His hand, as His working in my life toward positive and purposeful goals. None of these things, therefore, ever distressed, disappointed, or depressed me, though they may have greatly exercised my spirit. I have also come through years of evangelistic effort, missionary enterprise, Bible teaching ministry, and other and varied forms of Christian service, to realize that the Lord has been working out in me what He did within me way back on July 25, 1925, when He circumcised my heart that I might more fully love the Lord.

Life from that time has been a moving into His fuller purpose through a deeper meaning of the cross. Thus life has never been for me a going round in circles but a progressive on-going in which I have had no trust in myself but in God. And the first thing that affected me in those assemblies of believers commonly known as "brethren" was a new sense of freedom. I was the Lord's free man. Hitherto I had always been connected with, or joined to, or writing reports for, someone or something. Now I was the Lord's free man to serve Him and be answerable to Him alone.

The second thing was a new understanding of the church. The church is one: one fold, one family, one nation, one household, one temple, one pearl, one new man, one body. This is emphasized over and over in the Scriptures. But what is called Christendom here on earth is a multitudinous form of divisions and designations. There are

252

so many divisions, all penetrated through with so much suspicion and distrust. This earthiness of outlook, so prevalent now in Christendom, is due to the lack of spiritual perception, and that derives from a shallow, individual response to the principle of the cross and the authority of the Scriptures. Thus the church is viewed as a very earthy thing, whereas its origin is heavenly and eternal, something which was in the mind of God from eternity.

In my own ministry I have never denounced denominations. We should beware of a censorious spirit. For one thing, many of the Lord's dearest and choicest of saints are in various denominations. Also, I have never begged anyone to leave their denomination to fellowship with those who meet in the simplicity of the New Testament spirit. For unless these principles of gathering are seen spiritually—that is, by the illumination of the Spirit of God—they can never produce inward repose of spirit and spiritual satisfaction.

But within the bounds of that which is sectarian, by the very nature of things, there must be inevitable limitation and weakness, and positive hindrance to the Lord's full purpose. It is of little point for churches to boast in their increase of numbers or the work they accomplish. Thank God for that! And there is no doubt that the Lord is using the witness and testimony of every denomination that is truly Christian. But, surely, the very nature of the sectarian spirit, which excludes other believers unless they join up, or subscribe to, a certain creed, brings limitation and a measure of weakness (see 1 Cor. 1:10-13). The true assembly has no defined creed. The whole Word of God is the sole guiding principle for doctrine and conduct. If I may so say, then, my second benefit derived from fellowship with these assemblies has been clearer views of what the church really is.

The third is a new order of things. In assemblies where I fellowship the remembrance meeting takes precedence. It is a heart exercise of worship in spirit and in truth, expressed publicly, freely, and spontaneously, by the men of the fellowship taking leadership, although the sisters exercise themselves no less significantly in their worship to the Lord. The Lord's people are a royal and holy priesthood whose chief function is to offer "spiritual sacrifices unto God."

253

This is not the presentation of our bodies for service, nor intercession on behalf of others, but the expression of hearts filled with rapturous, adoring praise of Him whose boundless love has redeemed us. I have had such sight of the unutterable glories and the inexpressible loveliness of the Lord Jesus at these meetings that my soul has often been ravished with His love and drawn out in great affection toward Him. It is this worship at the heart of the assembly which issues in something which is described as doing things "decently and in order." There is a certain spiritual orderliness about the whole life of the assembly and its work and witness for the Lord when the worship and remembrance feast has its primary place.

The Lord's Supper gathers up all essential truth and testimony: our Lord's death for us; our death in Him; the oneness of believers as one loaf; our feeding on the Lord Jesus to gain strength for spiritual ongoing; and the joyous hope of His coming again. How important it is, therefore, to exercise ourselves in this, His own appointed way. Nothing can excel what the Lord Himself has arranged for us to do.

The elements of the Lord's Supper are passed hand to hand. There is no kneeling before men. In other services there are other emphases, such as for preaching the gospel or prayers for all men. There is no one-man ministry in true assembly life, but the development of spiritual gift in many, so that the Word of God is ministered both ably and adequately, with profit to the people of God.

The fourth thing I must mention is the family consciousness. There is a bond, holy, strong, and tender, which unites the whole family of God. It is the nearest feeling which earth knows to the immeasurable love of Christ to His church. I have found that this bond seems to have far fuller expression among the Lord's people in assemblies than in most other groups. In the first place, they are smaller and more closely knit groups compared to the large denominational churches. But it is rather that they seek to exercise themselves in the Scriptural principle of hospitality. Worldwide, I have found them to love each other most sincerely, to have a care of, and concern for, each other.

In a world which pours out volumes of base suspicion and distrust, how blessed it is, especially for those of us who are travelling to minister the Word of God, to be protected from this awful miasma by the sheltering care of godly homes and the loving care of dear sisters of God. In all these seventeen years of intense travel among assemblies in many lands, I have never been sent to a hotel. As a guest in hundreds of homes, I must set on record that our married sisters are, to my mind, some of the most consecrated portions of the Lord's people, whose roots are deep in godliness, and whose branches are laden with kindness, love, and care for all the Lord's people.

My Praise to God

I would not want to close the little story of my life without some praise of God and some expression of gratitude for what He has done for my soul. Love is the most sublime principle which man can know, and I am thankful for the measure of God's own love which has been shed abroad in me. There have been times, of course, when I have had to come before the Lord with little but confession, but my chief exercise has been one of worship, praise, and adoring love of Him.

I am grateful to God for giving me life and being as a human person; for the kind of home, in spite of its short-comings, into which I was born; for parents who nursed me through dependent years; for a healthy and strong physical frame and sound mind; for all the persons with whom I have lived, and the scores of places where my abode has been; for all friends who have enriched my life and given me so much comfort and joy; for delivering me out of many dangers in foreign lands; for bringing me from the chambers of illness, especially from surgery in China which had to be done without a general anaesthetic. But I am most grateful to be numbered with the host of His redeemed.

Such a review of my heavenly Father's mercies toward me bows my heart in grateful praise. Like David I can but say, "How great is the sum of them."